# A BRIEF MEMOIR OF
# THE MILDMAY FAMILY

# A BRIEF MEMOIR OF THE
# MILDMAY FAMILY

### COMPILED BY LIEUT.-COLONEL
### HERBERT A. ST. JOHN MILDMAY

PRIVATELY PRINTED
BY JOHN LANE THE BODLEY HEAD
LONDON AND NEW YORK.   MCMXIII

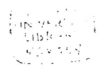

*One Hundred and Fifty copies only of this book*
*have been printed*

WILLIAM BRENDON AND SON, LTD., PRINTERS, PLYMOUTH

# PREFACE

THE Compiler regrets that after considerable trouble and research he has not been able to make the Mildmay Memoir more thorough and complete, nor to form a continuous story because the histories of the various members of the family rarely run one into the other. He can however assert that he has been careful not to make any statements for which there is not good warrant, and he hopes that the present and future members of the family, to whom the book is affectionately dedicated, will find something to interest them in this account of their ancestors. Lastly the Compiler wishes to acknowledge most gratefully the generous treatment accorded to him by the publisher Mr. John Lane, and the very kind and generous assistance of relatives and friends.

# CONTENTS

# ILLUSTRATIONS

B

# A BRIEF MEMOIR OF THE MILDMAY FAMILY

## ORIGIN OF FAMILY, MEANING OF NAME, AND ARMS

ONE writer has said that the Mildmay family came from Lancashire, and another that it came from the West of England ; but there is no certainty as to the place of origin. A suggestion has been made that the Mildmays did really belong to Essex, and originate from the hamlet of Middlemead in Little Baddow, in that county, which in Domesday is called Mildemet. This is possible, for when the family came prominently forward in the sixteenth century they were undoubtedly well-established Essex people living in the neighbourhood of Little Baddow.

The deed of Henry de Mildeme of about the year 1347 makes a gift of land from his manor of Stonhouse, Gloucestershire, which shows that at an early period one of the family lived in the West of England.

The name, like most others, has varied somewhat

in spelling, some of the variations being Mildeme, Mildemay, Myldmay, Milldmy, Milmay, etc.

In a deed of the 23rd March, 1599, for the maintenance of the children of Wm. Mildmay, the name is written Mildemaye, Myldemaie, Myldmay, and Myldemaye, four different ways in the same deed; but by the end of the seventeenth century the name seems to have settled down into its present form of Mildmay.

William Playfair, in *British Family Antiquity*, 1811, vol. vii, pp. 124, etc., writes of St. John-Mildmay :—
"The latter of the two names borne by the present family, that of Mildmay (anciently spelt Mildeme or Mildme), is evidently of Saxon origin, and is compounded of two Saxon words, Mild, soft or tender, and Dema, a judge, to which profession it is possible that one of the earliest members of the family may have belonged."

This explanation of the name seems farfetched, and is certainly not capable of proof, as the family cannot be traced in the history of Saxon times, nor any record found of a lawyer belonging to it earlier than in the Tudor period.

Barber puts :—" Mildmay, Mildmé, a French personal name," but gives no authority for his statement.

Robert Ferguson, in *English Surnames*, p. 248, has :—" The Anglo-Saxon Milde, mild, gentle, entered into several names of women—hence our name Mildred—we have also Mildmay, which has just the same meaning from May, a maid."

Mrs. Holt, who, over the signature of " Hermentrude," was a frequent contributor to *Notes and
Queries* on genealogy and kindred subjects, wrote
to us in a letter dated 14 June, 1892 :—

" Sir, my reasons for the conclusion that the
surname ' May ' is not derived from the month
but from ' maiden ' are these.

" (1) While nearly, if not quite, every day of the
week has originated a surname, no month of the year,
setting aside the two names that were under discussion, has been known to do so. We never met
with Mr. January, or Mrs. July.

" (2) May is a very common contraction of
maiden in mediæval times, as Halliwell's dictionary
will tell you.

" (3) The other names ending in ' May,' or
compounded with it, seem much more naturally
applicable to the maiden than to the month, e.g.
Fairmay, Sadmay, Le May (Le Mayden also occurs)
the masculine article merely indicating that the name
in that instance was borne by a man. Mildmay
therefore, I judge, should be rendered ' merciful
maiden,' that being the older meaning of mild.

" Allow me to remain,
" Yours faithfully,
" EMILY S. HOLT. ' Hermentrude.' "

At present, therefore, we can only say that no
definite conclusion can be arrived at as to place of
origin, or even of meaning of name.

An experienced professional genealogist who

made an exhaustive examination of a vast quantity
of matter, both printed and MS., referring to
periods prior to 1580, found much that was
interesting and important, but says in his report that
very little early genealogical information was forth-
coming, only revealing one Walter Mildmay, who
in the 1 Richard III was keeper of the park of
Morlewood.

Among the Fane papers belonging to the Earl
of Westmoreland, which we have seen, are some
very interesting ones referring to the Mildmays,
especially the earliest reported members of that
family.

One of these papers is an illuminated pedigree
on parchment of the Mildmays dated 1583, and
signed by the Earl Marshal and Robert Cooke;
but what is more important is, that there are a
number of ancient documents of various kinds,
enclosed in a quaint old leather-covered box, in
proof of almost all the first fifteen members in the
line of descent.

Walter Mildmay of Writtel, Essex, is stated in
the above-mentioned pedigree to have been of the
household of Anne, Duchess of Buckingham, and
this can be proved by *Liber providens magni
hospitii Annæ Ducissæ Buckingham anno regis Edward
vi, sexto*, a book that was in the Apethorpe library,
and this same book includes Thomas, Walter's
father, among the attendants on the Duchess.

In 1552 Sir Walter Mildmay of Apethorpe had
a grant of arms of a horse with wings, courant,

sable (Herald's office); but we have not found or heard of any document on which these arms are displayed.

Guillim in his *Heraldry*, 6th ed., 1724, p. 147, says :—"Azure on a Bend Argent, a Pegasus, volant, sable, was granted by Sir Gilbert Pethick, Garter, the 20th May, 6 Edward III, to Sir Walter Mildmay, Kt, of Essex, who was descended of a House undefamed, and had of long time used himself in Feats of Arms, and works vertuous."

The crest which was then also granted is on a Wreath or and gules, a Demi-Roebuck proper, with two wings Argent having about his Neck a collar, gules, bezanté, and the Ring and Horns Tipp'd or, mantled gules, doubled or.

Edward III in the above should be Edward VI. See Dallaway's *Heraldry*, p. liv.

Among the Fane papers is a confirmation on parchment of the ancient arms of Mildmay to Sir Walter Mildmay, Kt., Chancellor of the Exchequer to Queen Elizabeth, by Robert Cooke, and as this document is quaint as well as interesting, it is given at full length.

" To all and singular as well Nobles as others to whome theis preasantes shall come Robert Cooke Esquier, alias Clariencieulx principall Harrold and Kinge of Armes in the East, West and South partes of the Realme of Englande from River of Trent salutem. And it is dailie seene that tyme (destroyer and consumer of all thinges) throwes downe and extinguishes manie ancient and honorable families or by alteringe and translatinge their houses and habitacions obscures their worthie races and extractions that therebie God's justice maie be felte and manne's patience tryed : so comes it to passe as often that the same tyme (mother of treuthe) bringeth to light and discovereth to be gentlemen of longe and auncient continuewance divers whose auncestors (sundrie yeares before) weare not reputed of such antiquitie that thereby the same God's mercie maie be seene and his bountie praised. And this to be soe I finde preasantly manifested in the Stocke or Lineage whereof Sir Walter Mildemay K$^t$ Chauncellor of the Exchequire and of the Queene's Mat most honourable Privie Councell is discended. For proofe whereof this daie has his sonne and heire apparent Anthony Mildemay an Esquier of Her Mat Stable shewed unto mee (in the presence of divers other Harroldes) such auncient credible and authentical deedes charters recordes writinges evidences and letters some sealed with seales of Armes as well of theire Auncestors as of divers noble Earles Barrons and other greate personages of this Lande namely of Simon S$^t$ Lize Earle of Huntingdon and Northampton of Gb$^{te}$ Marshall Earle of Pembroke of Thomas Hollande Earle of Kent and Duke of Surrey of Edmund and Humphrey Earles of Stafford of Richard Nevell Earl of Warwicke of Anne Nevell Duchess of Buckingham and of John Abbot of Evesham.

" As notwithstandinge anie doubte that mighte growe through length of tyme or ignorance of

evidence it appears clearlie that the saide Sir Walter
is by fourteene discents (from father to sonne)
lynally and lawfully extracted of the bodie of
a verie auncient gentleeman of this lande
called Hugh Mildemay[1] whoe (witnesse a deede
of the saide Earle Symon) lived aboute Kinge
Stephen's tyme now four hundreth—and—yeares
paste, and had issue one Sir Robert Mildemay[2]
K[t] and—one Rogier[3] and this another Rogier[4] a
K[t] and Henry de Mildemay Senior[5] then hee one
Raphe de Mildemay[6] and hee another Raphe[7]
and this Raphe Henry de Mildemay[8] Junior
and hee one Robert de Mildemay[9] and hee another
Robert[10] whoe had issue Thomas Mildemay[11]
father to Walter Mildemay[12] whoe was the first of
that S[r]name being an officer in the said Duchess of
Buckingham's house at Writtle in Essex that came
out of the West and dwelt in that Countie, wheare
he left issue Thomas Mildemay[13] of Chelmsford
in Essex father to Thomas[14] Mildemay of Mulsham
to William of Springfeelde in the same Countie to
John of Cretinghame in Suffolk and to this Sir
Walter of Apthorpe in the countie of Northampton
K[t], and as the continewance of this saide gentleman's house—discente thereof (witnesse the evidence and charters aforesaide) most directe and true
beinge verie probable to have been gentlemen longe
before the farthest tyme afore recited so it is as—
the above named Henry de Mildemay Junior nowe
remaininge in the—at their deedes amongst the
evidences aforesaide—pertaineth propperly to the

same house and familie.   For theis two being greate grand father one to the other—script with their propper names and S^rnames, three Lyons rompinge which bee azure in a fielde silver, for none else in this lande gives the same : as by most diligente searche made in—the Registers of myne office is to be sene and proved.   And therefore beinge there-untoe requested heere I have delivered under my hande and seale of myne office the said armes, as in the margente hereof depicted more plainlie is showed.   Further for the better continewance thereof in memorie I have subscribed a pedigree (bearing this date) whearein orderly and verbatim bee enrolled all the saide deedes charters writinges and maniments in the custodie (as is aforesaide) of the saide Sir Walter.   Unto whome and his heires and to the heires of his father by power and authoritie to me committed by letters pattentes under the greate Seale of Englande and by virtue of myne office aforesaide, I doe by this preasantes Restore Ratify and Confirm the saide Armes that is to say the feelde argente three lyons rompinge azure that hee and they the same maie beare use and shewe forth in shielde cote armour or otherwise with their due difference, at his or their pleasures according to their auncient and true righte without impediment, lett, contradiction, challenge or inter-ruption of any persone or persones whatsoever.

"Dated at London the twentieth of August, Anno Domini 1583 and in the Five and twentieth yeare of the reigne of Our Sovreigne Ladye Elizabeth by the Grace of God of Englande, France, and Irelande Queene.    "Defender of the Faith.

"Be it further remembered that like as the saide familie of Mildemay there dooth, as it is before declared belonge of greate antiquitie this coate of three lyons rampant azure in argent: Even so through longe processe of tyme the same growinge, as is above noted, to decay and the Armes forgotten, in the Reigne of the late moste noble Prince Kinge Henrie the Eigth—familie by the goodness of Almightie God being raised upp againe, there was given unto Thomas Mildemay of Chelmsforde, and untoe his posteritie by my then predecessor a Coate of Armes, viz :—Silver and Sable (onde per) fesse three Greyhound heades cuppé, with collars gules purflied or, which Coate by reason of the saide grante is lawfully discended to all ye children of ye saide Thomas Mildemay of Chelmsforde, and therefore I the said Clariencieulx nowe Kinge at Armes dooe by theis preasantes testify and declare that the above named Sir Walter Mildemay K$^t$ and all the children and posteritie of the saide Thomas Mildemay of Chelmsforde his father may (with their due difference) lawfully and rightlie beare as well ye saide newe as ye oulde depicted and quartered, as ye see in the margent of this Codicell written the daye and yeare of Her Maj$^{tie}$ aforesaide.

"Robert   Cooke   (alias   Clariencieulx)   Roy d'Armes."

There are a few illegible words in the above confirmation but not enough to obscure the meaning,
and the whole put shortly means that the Herald
predecessor of Robert Cooke had granted to
Thomas Mildmay of Chelmsford, father of Sir
Walter, a coat of arms of three greyhound heads,
which arms the descendants of Thomas were
entitled to use.    Further, that he, Robert Cooke, had
confirmed to Sir Walter what he calls the ancient
arms of the family of three lions rampant.    They
are called the ancient arms because they are on the
seal of a deed of Henry de Mildeme of about the
year 1300, and can be plainly seen to this day on
the seal of that deed.    The first sealed Mildmay
deed is that of Herbert Mildeme of about the year
1270, and this shows one lion only.

Sir Walter used the arms of the three greyhound
heads, for they are to be seen on the seal of a deed
by which he bequeathed to Christ's Hospital an
annuity of £2 12s. charged on two messuages in the
parish of St. Botolph, Aldersgate, dated 10th April,
1556.

In Sir Walter's coat were for Le Rous, Argent,
on a canton gules, a mullet or ;  and for Cornish,
sable, a chevron embattled or, between three roses
argent.

In the *Encyclopædia Heraldica*, 1828, Berry
mentions a family of Mildmar with the same arms
of three lions rampant, but unfortunately does not
say to what county they belonged.

# FOUR THOMAS MILDMAYS

THE Rev. Edward Betham in his *Baronet-age* relates that a Mildmay is supposed to have accompanied King Richard I to the Holy Land, and a writer in the *Globe* of the 27th April, 1906, states that the person who had charge of the baggage of King John when it was lost in crossing the Wash was a knight of the name of Mildmay. Both these statements may be correct, but we have not been able to find any confirmation of them in the many histories and records we have searched, though as Robert Cooke says the Mildmays were very possibly "Gentlemen of long and ancient descent."

One Walter Mildmay, as before stated, is mentioned in the reign of Richard III, but except for this the ancient documents referred to as proving the descent tell the little that is known about the family before the time of four successive Thomas Mildmays, the first being Thomas Mildmay of Chelmsford, Essex, who married Agnes Reade, and in his will, dated 1547, describes himself as Yeoman and Merchant. He had several children, but directly or indirectly only mentions four in his will, namely, Thomas, William, John, and Walter.

One son, Edward, predeceased him, and in his will describes himself as of London, gentleman.   He is no doubt the Edward referred to in this note.

"Cordwaner Strett.   Edward Myldemay, son of Thomas Myldemay of Chelmesford, Co. Essex, yeoman, who was apprentice of Christopher Campion, citizen and mercer of London, was admitted into the liberty of the City of London, 6th Oct: 33 Hen: VIII."

In one clause of Thomas's will of 1547 there is left to the son William, " one stall in which I used to stand every Wednesday."

The market rights of Chelmsford belonged to the Mildmays till quite recently, when they were purchased by the town from the late Sir Henry St. John-Mildmay.

Thomas I did not belong to the Court of Augmentations, as stated in the D.N.B., but was evidently a man of some position, and had a grant in the 29th year of King Henry VIII of five tenements in the town of Chelmsford of an annual value of £6 11s. 2d., for a knight's service, an annual payment of 13s. 2d. and a consideration of £79 6s. 8d.

Also, as before stated, he had a grant of arms. The Reade family into which he married was also armigerous, so the combined influence was able to advance the fortunes of his son Thomas, who is the first to be mentioned in public affairs, and through whom came great increase of wealth to the family, and its consequent rise in influence and importance.

This Thomas, the second of the four, married

CHELMSFORD

Avicia or Hawise Gunson, who brought him as part of her dowry a chapel belonging to the Abbey of St. Oswith and its tithes, valued then at £5 per ann.; and the appurtenances and moiety of the tithes of Moulsham, belonging to the same Abbey, and granted by King Henry VIII to her father William Gunson, Treasurer of the Marine Causes.

Thomas II was Auditor of the Court of Augmentations and of the Duchy of Cornwall in the reign of King Henry VIII, at the time of the suppression of the Monasteries, which office gave him ample opportunities for enriching himself and acquiring large estates in the County of Essex and elsewhere.

Here we may insert a little extract referring to the position of Auditor from B.M. Arundel MS. 151, fol. 386.

"This much is certain that a great number of men who when appointed to the office were possessed only of inkhorn and pen, were, after two years, able to rank in wealth and estate with the highest in the land."

Thomas the Auditor is a case in point.

On 20 July, 1540, Thomas Mildemaye, one of the Auditors of the Court of Augmentation, and Avicia his wife, grant in fee for £622 5s. 8d. (twenty years' purchase) of the manor of Mulsham, Essex, with the watermill of Mulsham, and all appurtenances in Chelmsford, Mulsham, Magna Baddowe, Stokk, Wydforde, and Writell in Essex, which belonged to the late Monastery of St. Peter's,

Westminster, as fully as William Boston, the late
Abbot, held it. Rent £4 14s. with liberties,
and fee, except for some small charges amounting
to £1 2s. yearly. Altogether about 1800 acres.
There was a house of Black Friars at Moulsham
valued at the dissolution at £9 6s. 5d. a year.
Mulsham appears as Molesham in Domesday, was
sometimes written Mowsham, and later on became
Moulsham.

The mansion of Moulsham was built by Thomas
Mildmay of so grand a character that, as one writer
says :—" It was then accounted the greatest
Esquire's building in the County of Essex ";
and :—" In the said manor are many fair gardens
and orchards replenished with great store of good
and some rare kinds of fruits and herbs. There
belong to it a dove house of brick, a fair game of
deer unparked, a great warren, a good fishing
course both in private pond and common river, a
very good watermill, and very greate store of
other necessary provisions."

Though the Auditor is believed to have built in
1542-3, he possibly did not do so till some years
after acquiring the property, for in the early years
of the reign of King Henry VIII the houses
of country gentlemen were thatched buildings,
walls covered with the coarsest clay, and lighted
only by lattices.

Harrison, writing in the time of Queen Elizabeth,
says :—" Such as be latelie builded are commonly
of brick or stone, or both, their rooms large and

THOMAS MILDMAY, AUDITOR OF THE COURT OF AUGMENTATIONS

comelie, and houses of offices further distant from
their lodgings." Windows, interior decorations,
and furniture also improved, and became more
useful and ornamental.

To continue the Auditor's acquisitions.  On the
24th November, 1540, grant by King Henry VIII
to Thomas Mildemaye of the House and College
of Acon in the City of London.  Term twenty-one
years, rent £3 6s. 8d.  Pennant does not mention
house or College, but says the Church and Cloisters
were granted by King Henry VIII to the Mercers'
Company and became Mercers' Hall.

Once more in 1540, Annuity arising out of the
manor of Isleworth from the Abbess and Convent
of Syon.

Then, on 14 February, 1541, to Morgan
Philippe, *alias* Wolf, Goldsmith, one of the
Stewards of the Chamber, and Elizabeth his wife.
Licence to alienate a tenement called Rynged Hall,
and four tenements on the highway on the west
side of the entrance of the said tenement, in the
parish of St. Thomas the Apostle in London,
which belonged to Bewlay Abbey, near Oxford,
to Thomas Mildemaye, of London.

The Auditor also bought the manor of Little
Waltham, and in May, 1587, there were licences
for selling the property to different people.

The manors of Great Leighs and Bishops Leighs
he purchased from Thomas Howard, Duke of
Norfolk, and these his heirs sold.  Waltham and
the two Leighs were in Essex.

c

Other properties, more or less important, he became possessed of, as is shown in his will, but he does not seem to have been always over-burdened with cash, for his father-in-law, William Gunson, writing to him 11 August, 1542, says :—
"Loving son at this point I have had your letter written this day at Chellmysford, and perceive you have command to prepare 20 footmen, and that you would be holpen with bows and arrows, and bills if you lack any, and that I shall write to you how you shall act, and whether you shall prepare coats for the men. Although the preparation for 20 be much, you must needs do it, and as for bows &c. I am compelled to buy for myself and so must you, and I suppose you must prepare coats."

In 1558 he was Sheriff of Essex, and in 1560, acting in that capacity, he committed Anne Dowe for asserting that Queen Elizabeth was in child by Robert Duddeley, for which the punishment was standing in the pillory, having the ears cut off, and perhaps a portion of the tongue.

In Chelmsford is a free grammar school, founded and endowed in 1552 on the petition of Thomas Mildmay, Sir Walter Mildmay, and others ; and in Moulsham are six Almshouses erected by Thomas Mildmay in 1565, and rebuilt by Sir William Mildmay in 1758. There is a quaint Mildmay endowment to these Almshouses, viz. the distribution of an ox or bullock amongst the poor people of Chelmsford on Christmas Eve, and £3 6s. 8d. to buy three barrels of white herrings

and four cades of red herrings for distribution
amongst the poor people of Moulsham and Chelmsford the first and second week of clean Lent. A
cade was a barrel containing six hundred herrings.
This endowment is now used for the purchase of
coals.

At Dogmersfield is the Queen's general pardon
to Thomas Mildmay, Auditor, dated 1 Mary,
October 3.

The Auditor died 21 September, 1566, and
was buried at Chelmsford on the 26th. He left
instructions in his will :—"that his executors shall
erect a stone monument within the Church wall at
Chelmsford to the value of £40, engraven with
my arms and those of my wife, with the pictures
of both, and 15 children, one half men children
and one half women children."

The mathematical instruction is not very accu-
rate, but the monument is in Chelmsford Church,
and the "picture" on it shows the old Auditor
kneeling with eight sons behind him, and Avice,
his wife, with seven daughters behind her.

The monument resembles a sarcophagus in
design, the lower part of fine early Elizabethan
work, the upper portion a later addition, very
inferior and not in harmony with the lower. Date
about 1571. The arms on it are the three greyhound heads couped. This monument formerly
stood in the north chancel in the Mildmay Chapel,
from whence it was moved. Old Chelmsford
Church once bore on the outside of the south wall

the following inscription :—"Prey for the good estate of the township of Chelmsford, that hath been willing and prompt of helpys to build this Church.   M.C.C.C.LXXXIX."   This was lost when that side of the church fell down in 1800.

Avice, the Auditor's wife, predeceased him, for she died in 1557, and we find in Machyn's diary for that year :—"The v daye of October was bered at Chernford in Essex, the wyff of Thomas Myldmay, sqwyre and audetor, with ij whytt branchys, and ij dozen of gret staffe torchys, and iii dozen of stockyons, and many mourners in blake."

According to the Chelmsford registers the 5 October should be the 10th.

The Auditor's eldest son, Thomas, third of the name, succeeded him at Moulsham.   He was dubbed Knight by Robert, Earl of Leicester 23 June, 1566 ; was Sheriff, 1568 ; Deputy-Lieutenant, 1572 ; and M.P. for Essex, 1585.   He had much to do with raising and commanding the train bands, the county being able to furnish 12,000 men.   Robert Wrothe, writing to him 5 March, 1587, begs to be relieved from mustering and certifying by the 18th of the month, as this is but "Scarborough warning" for him, i.e. no warning at all.

In this Sir Thomas's time Queen Elizabeth on her progress into Essex and Suffolk slept four nights at Moulsham, beginning 7 September, 1579.

That somewhat uncertain sovereign apparently

held him in high favour, for in Strype's *Annals* for 1594 we find :—

"Among many good Princes, Her Majesty's manly progenitors, and in other well governed Commonwealths at this day, joining Policy with Pity, it hath been and is reputed great wisdom to provide means, that the certain number of Foreigners coming to inhabit this our Country or any other, and the several occasions of their coming, might be certainly known by notorious and perfect registers, kept in some special office to be appointed for that purpose, of what nation each Foreigner were, the cause of his coming, his calling and condition, Art and Science, when and where he arrived, in what place he inhabited, and what time he returned again to his own country.

"It may now so please Her Majesty of her special Grace and favour, for these necessary reasons ensuing, for the yearly rent of £40 to be paid into Her Highness' Court of Exchequer, and in consideration of the true and faithful Service done unto Her Majesty for the space of twenty eight years now past by Sir Thomas Mildmay, Knight, Her Grace's servant, to erect an office for that purpose by Her Highness' Letters Patent, making and ordaining him the said Sir Thomas, Officer thereof, granting unto him and his Assigns Power and Authority thereby for the term of 21 years, to begin from the Feast of the Birth of Our Lord God last past, to make and keep a register of the Names, Ages, and Abilities of Body,

Countries, Callings, Arts, Sciences, Places of Habitation, Causes of repair hither, and time of departure hence of all Foreigners and Strangers, now being and inhabiting within Her Highness' Realm of England, and of all others that shall from time to time come into this Realm to inhabit, or pass forth from the same, during the same period of 21 years, except all Ambassadors and their Trains, Noblemen, or Gentlemen, Ladies or Gentlewomen, coming of pleasure to see Her Majesty and her Realm, and Scots.

"Allowing the said Sir Thomas or his Assigns, for the first entry after, during the continuance of the said term, fourpence for every poll for such as be Householders, and twopence the poll for Children and Servants, and fourpence the poll for everyone that shall depart the Realm again."

Then follow the reasons for creating this office, concluding with :—"There be few or no poor people among them, so as it can not be justly intended that this Payment of 6d. (*sic*) for the first entry and 4d. and 2d. yearly after as aforesaid, can not (*sic*) be offensive. And it is very evidently seen and known that after they be once settled here they become wealthy in short space however poor and needy they were at their first coming. Therefore the Burthen being so small to them nothing being taken from any of our own Nation, but so many benefits growing to the Realm by the means of erecting the said Office, and a yearly Revenue coming to the Crown thereby, it may therefore please Her Most Excellent Majesty to favour this humble petition of the said Sir Thomas, and to grant the same accordingly."

All this would seem to indicate a fairly large ingress and egress of Foreigners in and out of England, for allowing £20 as the expense of carrying on the office, Sir Thomas would have had to disburse £60 yearly, and this would mean that 2700 adults at fourpence, and 1800 children or servants at twopence, would have to arrive in or depart from the country before he could derive any benefit from the Act.

Perhaps it was to look after the affairs of this office that he went to London, for in the entries of strangers resident in London in 1595, there appears Sir Thomas Mildmay of Mowsome, Essex, in Allgate Ward.

Whether the Alien Act was beneficial or not, it was, at any rate, considerably easier for a despotic sovereign in the sixteenth century to establish it, than for a Prime Minister in the twentieth; easier, too, to carry it out when passed.

In 1591 a survey of Chelmsford was taken for Sir Thomas, and in this is stated :—" Chelmsforde is one ancient goodly manor, situate in the hearte of the country in good and wholesome air, conveniently and well housed, and well built for timber and tile. The chief manor house was in the time of Edward the Therde brent and wasted with fire ; and before it seemed to have been some ancient Barony. Within this manor is situate the town of Chelmesforde, well situated with more than 300 habitations, divers of them seemly for gentlemen ; many fair inns, and the residue of the same habitations for victuallers and artificers of city-like buildings. This town is called the Shire town, not only by the Statute of Henry VII for the custody of weights and measures, but so reputed and taken long time before by the keeping of all Assizes and Sessions of the Peace."

Of this Sir Thomas, who died in 1608, there is a half-length portrait in armour at Dogmersfield, and at the same place a fine full-length one in robes of his father, the Auditor.

Sir Thomas married, first, Lady Frances Radcliff, daughter of Henry, Earl of Sussex, by whom he had a large family, and this marriage brought valuable property into the family, as is shown in the account of Sir Henry St. John-Mildmay.

The second wife of Sir Thomas was Margaret, daughter of Richard Whethill, of London, by whom he had an illegitimate son, Walter, which is probably the reason why she is generally omitted from the pedigree.

Sir Thomas was succeeded by his son Thomas, the fourth of that name, Sheriff of Essex in 1609. He was created Baronet 29 June, 1611 ; married, firstly, Elizabeth, daughter of Sir John Puckering, Lord Chancellor of England, and secondly, 16 March, 1616, Anne Saville, by whom he had three daughters, but died without male issue in 1625.

# SIR HENRY MILDMAY OF
# WOODHAM WALTERS

THE heir to the fourth Thomas Mildmay was his brother Sir Henry of Woodham Walters, Sheriff of Essex, 1629, who married Elizabeth, daughter and coheir of Thomas Darcye of Toleshunt Darcye. The name of Walters came from the FitzWalters, who formerly owned the property.

Sir Henry was a claimant for the FitzWalter Barony, as is more fully related in the account of the FitzWalters.

In the time of this Sir Henry an interesting event is recorded as taking place at Moulsham. John Reeve writes :—"1 November 1638/9. Uppon Monday last the King waited on by the Lords and the rest of the Court went from hence to Chensford and next day to Mousum to Sir Henry Milema's where the Queene Mother had been lodged the night before. Shee mett hym below the Stayres in the Hall near the Screene ledd by my Lord Goring, where after the King had bowd towards the hemme of her garment then rising towards her hand kissed her who held him a great while uppon her neck without speaking to him."[1]

The above agrees very well with the account in

[1] Denbigh Papers, Hist. MS. Com.

a little book or pamphlet by P. de la Serre, en-
titled, *Histoire de l'Entrée de la Reine Mère dans la
Grande Bretagne.* In this there is an engraving of
Moulsham, which shows a castellated structure
walled round, with moat and drawbridge, and pictures the meeting in 1639 of King Charles I and
Marie de' Medici in the outer Courtyard, thus
described, (translated from the French) page 19 :—
"Her Majesty left this fine house (St. John's
Abbey, Colchester) to sleep near the town of
Chelmsford in a castle belonging to M. de Mildmay,
a Knight of importance, as well for his own merit,
as from the antiquity of his noble race."

Then follows a description of how the Queen
and her suite were lodged and entertained, and at
page 22 the report continues :—"The next day the
Queen being ready to leave, and just about to quit
her room and get into her coach, was informed
that the King her son-in-law had arrived and was
entering the Castle, which obliged the Queen to
descend more promptly from her room to the door
of the Hall where one passed into the Courtyard,
where the King meeting the Queen, who came
towards him, after saluting him, kissed her."

It is this supreme moment that is shown in the
engraving ; but this engraving is in one point
strangely at variance with the description of the
house given in Morant's Essex, for the engraving
distinctly shows a moat filled with water, and
Morant says :—"The manor is seated—on sand and
gravel not moated or encompassed with water."

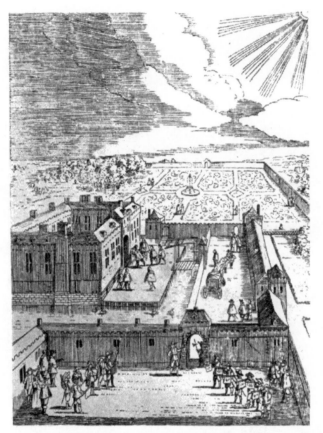

MOULSHAM HALL, AS BUILT BY THOMAS MILDMAY

# SIR HENRY MILDMAY OF GRACES, HIS SONS AND GRANDSONS

THOMAS the Auditor had several brothers. One was John, owner of Creatingham, Suffolk, and Terling, Essex, who died in 1580. His eldest son was John, and his line finished with Robert in the fourth generation.

Terling was bought by the Auditor in 1563, passed to his brother John, then to John's second son Robert, and from him to his cousin Robert, who married his second cousin Cecilia Haynes, a widow, daughter of Sir Humphrey Mildmay of Danbury, and they left six daughters, who sold the property to Thomas Western. Cecilia's portrait was at Danbury, and came into the possession of the late Mr. Edgar Disney, member of a family that at one time owned Danbury.

Another of the Auditor's brothers was William, seated at Springfield Barnes, Essex. This had been held by Coggeshall Abbey, and, coming to the Crown, was granted by King Edward VI to William Mildmay with other lands, and a chantry founded by Margaret Coggeshall in Baddow Church worth yearly £20 16s. 8d.

William's manor-house stood near the river as

you go from Chelmsford to Little Baddow, and
perhaps it was the picturesque old gabled house,
with groups of clustered chimneys, still standing
near the ruins of the old Cistercian Abbey.

William, who died 13 February, 1570, married
a daughter of Pascall of Much Baddow, and had a
son, Thomas, who was Sheriff of Essex in 1597,
and was knighted in 1603 at the coronation of
King James I. He married Agnes or Alice Winthrop of Groton, Suffolk, the names being written
Graveton and Winthrope in very old pedigrees, and
in one deed we have seen Wyntroppe of Grafton.

We believe Agnes to have been a daughter of
Adam Winthrop, but she is variously described as
his daughter, widow, and sister. Sir Thomas died
in 1612 ; his eldest son was William, referred to
later on, and his second Thomas, who extinguished
himself by marrying a chambermaid from the household of the Earl of Sussex.

The marriage of Thomas and Agnes brought
the family into connection with John Winthrop,
first Governor of Massachusetts, and there are
letters to the Governor referring to his cousin Sir
Henry Mildmay of Graces, third son of Thomas
and Agnes.

At Boston, U.S.A., is preserved a stoneware pot,
" tipped and covered with a silver lydd," given by
Lady Mildmay, wife of Sir Thomas, to her brother
the Governor.

Lucy, Governor Winthrop's youngest sister,
married Emmanuel, son of Edmund Downing,

one of the signers in 1585 of the Statutes of Emmanuel College.

Emmanuel, Lucy's husband, was the father of Sir George Downing, and in *London Past and Present*, published in 1909, there is the following :—

"Downing Street is named after Sir George Downing, soldier and politician, who served both Cromwell and Charles II, and received from the latter a grant of land at Whitehall and a Baronetcy, and whose grandson founded Downing College, Cambridge. Born about 1623, son of Emmanuel Downing of the Inner Temple, at the age of about fifteen he accompanied his parents to New England and finished his education at Harvard, of which he was second graduate, if not the first. In one of his farewell speeches in 1905 Mr. Rufus Choate, the popular American Minister (*sic*) to this country, claimed Downing as an American, and humorously commented on the vileness which enabled him to ingratiate himself successively with Cromwell, with the Rump Parliament, and with Charles II. If, he said, America seriously wishes to annex him, England may be well content to surrender this unlovely compound of servility, disloyalty, and stinginess, whose character was so well understood in New England that the common expression there for a false man was an 'arrant George Downing.'"

Lucy Downing was much with the Mildmays of Graces, and in one of her letters to her brother the Governor, she writes :—"Sir Henry Mildmay is much worn with the gout. We left him in a sore fit a week since and he takes it not kindlie that he hath no letter from you. He thinks it answers not the confidence he did put in you, my Lady received hers when we were thear." In another letter:—"I received your kind letter and your daintie fruits which were indeed as good as old England itself affords in their kinde, and we being at Graces I sent for them thither and Sir Henry and my Lady wear much taken with them. Sir Henry profest it did much satisfy him that things did prosper so well with you."

Sir Henry was Member for Maldon in 1625, 1627, and 1639, and Sheriff of Essex in 1628.

He married twice, and the fine monument to him and his two wives is in Little Baddow Church. He is in armour, lying down leaning on his arm that rests on a pillow, and under a dome supported by black marble pillars. On the base the two wives kneeling : one represents an elderly lady in hood and scarf, the other a young one superbly dressed, the whole in white alabaster in best Italian Renaissance style. The inscriptions on the tomb are in Latin and English. That in Latin reads :—
"Here are interred the remains of Henry Mild-may of Graces in Baddow in the County of Essex. He was a Soldier in the Irish wars, and was there honoured with the degree of Knighthood in the Field. His first wife was Alicia, the daughter of William Harris of Crixie, Knight, of the same county, by whom he had 3 daughters, Alice, Mary, and Frances. His second wife was Amy, daughter of

Brampton Gurdon, Esqre, of Accrington, in the County of Suffolk, by whom he had 2 sons, Henry and Walter, and one daughter, Elizabeth. He died on Wednesday the ninth of October, in the year of Our Lord, 1639, aged 61."

The English inscription is :—

"Eques auratus, well may he be sayd
  Whose coyne, not warlick courage, such hath made,
  But unto Mildmay, Miles we afforde
  As Knighted on the Field by his flesht sworde
  that Sworde which Tyme shall never sheathe in rust
  but hangs it as a Trophy on his dust."

From the English inscription we may gather that at one time Sir Henry's sword was lying on or suspended over his tomb, and both the English and Latin inscriptions declare he was knighted in the field, but Metcalfe, in his *Book of Knights*, says he was knighted at Dublin Castle, 25 May, 1605, Sir Arthur Chichester being Lord Deputy.

He was probably knighted for some deed in one of the rebellions in Ireland that Sir Arthur Chichester fomented and Sir Henry Mildmay was active in suppressing.

Alicia, Sir Henry's first wife, brought the estate of Burnham into the family.

After more than four hundred years the tradition still lingers in the countryside that Sir Henry was not kind to Alicia, and that she drowned herself in a pond, now weedgrown and nearly silted up, that one passes when driving through a gateway in a stone wall close to Graces.

According to Mather, William, a son of Sir Henry Mildmay of Graces, with Mr. Lyon as tutor or attendant, was sent over from England to be educated at Harvard College. From the Steward's account-book it appears that he and Mr. Lyon continued at the college till 1651. William was ranked lowest in his class, but took his A.M. degree in regular course in 1647.

Sir Henry did not have a son named William, so doubtless Oldmixon is right in his *British Empire in America*, when he states that the William in question was "elder brother to Henry Mildmay Esqre of Shawford." Henry's elder brother was named William, and the dates suit.

Sir Henry's successor at Graces, his elder son Henry, was a bigoted Puritan, having been educated at Felsted School by Martin Holbeach, who had charge of the three sons of Oliver Cromwell.

In the Rebellion Henry commanded No. 50 troop of horse under the Earl of Bedford, having Robert Mildmay as his Cornet, and he was Governor of Cambridge Castle, where he promptly quarrelled with his Deputy-Governor, Captain Jordan.

He is most probably the Captain Mildmay referred to by Markham in his *History of the Great Lord Fairfax*, as having joined Lord Fairfax when that General advanced to the attack on Leeds, which began Monday, 23 January, 1643, when Captain Mildmay, with a company of dragooners, about 30 musketeers, and 100 clubmen, took up a position on Hunslet Moor, about half a mile from the town.

Henry sat in the Parliaments of Oliver and Richard Cromwell, in 1654, 56, and 59, and after the Restoration was elected a Member for Essex with Sir Fr. Masham, in 1689. He is often mentioned in the Autobiography of Sir John Bramston, who was at deadly enmity with him.

The Puritan soldier did not become a courtier, for he, with Sir Gobert Barrington and others, presented to King Charles II a petition from Essex concerning the Parliament. His Majesty did not receive it well, and said there were some would do well to remember the Act of Oblivion, and to take such courses as might not need another. That he very well remembered forty, and he turned away saying:—" Mr. Mildmay, I would you would remember forty." To which he very insolently replied:—" Sir, I remember sixty."

*Colonel* Henry, as he is called by contemporary writers, does not seem to have made himself generally agreeable, for in the Verney Memoirs we read :—
" We hear that Sir Edward Turner at the election (in Sussex) pulled Mildmay by the nose and otherwise affronted him, for which he said he would complain to Parliament, and further said that since he was hated by all the gentlemen in the country he would make them fear him. One of his friends has since fought Sir Ed: Turner and run him through the body, as 'tis reported here."

Colonel Mildmay, though not loyal to his King,

D

was loyal to his country. In 1698, when France
had declared war against the States General, they
appealed to England for assistance, to which by
treaty they were entitled. A mutiny arose among
the English troops ordered to the front, which
caused considerable alarm in England, and
Macaulay records in his *History of England* that
the matter being discussed in Parliament:—"'Write
to the Sheriffs,' said Colonel Mildmay, the member
for Essex, 'raise the Militia. There are a hundred
and fifty thousand of them : they are good Englishmen. They will not fail you.'"

The Republican Colonel died 13 December,
1692, and was buried at Little Baddow. His first
wife was Cecilia, daughter of Walter Barker of
Salop ; his second wife his cousin Mary, daughter
of Robert Mildmay of Overton, Northamptonshire, of which place Robert became possessed by
inheritance from his wife. One wishes when reading Robert's will that the jewels mentioned in it
had been preserved in the family.

Mary, the Republican's second wife, died
15 April, 1715, aged 78, and was buried at Little
Baddow. Graces passed to one of the four
daughters of Henry and Mary, who married
Edmund Waterson.

Little Baddow and Graces, in Essex, and
Creatingham, in Suffolk, were properties obtained
through the Court of Augmentations.

Baddow means bad water, on account of the
danger at the ford in flood time.

GRACES

No traces of Mildmay habitations are to be found at any of these places, except at Graces, where there are considerable remains. An end wall of the house showing the Elizabethan windows now blocked up, some of the front, parts of the old oak staircase and panelling, long stretches of wall, some being terrace or garden walls, some parts of a building with portions of two bay windows.

Graces was named after the old family of De Gras, to whom it had belonged, and must have been quite a large place.

# SIR WALTER MILDMAY OF
# APETHORPE

THE most famous of the brothers of the
Auditor was Walter, generally styled of
Apethorpe, Northamptonshire.

He was born in 1520 or 1521, and
his birthplace is believed to have been Chelmsford.

The first public mention of him is in a note
dated 9 June, 1540, in the account-book of the
Court of Augmentations, which is authenticated
thus :—" Extr: per me Wa Mildemay." So he must
have been in Government employ at an early age.

The next notice we have found of him is in
May, 1543, when he was appointed with Fra.
Southwell to be jointly and severally in survivor-
ship, Auditor of Accounts of the King's ships and
of all money expended in the King's affairs, with
£40 a year.

He was in the Exchequer in the reign of King
Edward VI, by whom he was made a Knight of
the Carpet 22 February, 1546.

Appointed Commissioner for the sale of Chancery
lands 17 April, 1548.

In 1551 he superintended the erection of a new
Mint at York.

In 1552 was directed to settle with the Crown

Accountants the effect of a fall in the value of money, and in the same year supervised the receipt by the Crown of plate, jewels, bells, etc., surrendered by the suppressed monasteries.

At the burial of Edward VI he was allowed nine yards of cloths, and his servants nine yards.

He was Member for Peterborough in the reign of Queen Mary, and although almost a Calvinist was employed by her and appointed Treasurer for the wars beyond the seas, in which service he went to the siege of Calais.

Later he became Principal Counsellor, Sub-Chancellor, and Under-Treasurer of the Exchequer to Queen Elizabeth, and was sworn of the Privy Council 17 July, 1566. He succeeded as Sub-Chancellor Sir Richard Sackville, who died in 1556, and he became Chancellor 5 February, 1588-9, the letters patent appointing him being among the Fane papers, and they carry a seal of Queen Elizabeth in fine condition.

He was never in sufficiently good Royal favour to reach the highest preferment, though Lodge says he was a candidate for the Seals.

Sir Walter studied the law, in which he became proficient, and is said to have been the person who first hit upon the method of cutting off an entail.

Sir Walter was educated at Christ's College, Cambridge, to which college he was a benefactor, and established there a Greek lecture of which Mede was the Reader for many years.

Furthermore, Richard Culverwell, mercer, and

Laurence Chaderton, Bachelor of Divinity, acting for him, purchased for £550 from Robert Taylor of Badburgham, who had inherited it from W. Sherwoode, the site at Cambridge of a dissolved house of Black Friars, and there Sir Walter founded and endowed in 1583-4 a new college called Emmanuel, the foundation being sufficient to maintain a Master, three Fellows, and four Scholars.

Sir Walter gave to the College houses in Bishopsgate Street, now very valuable ; land at Barking, Essex, which curiously enough brings the same rent of £20 a year that it did when gifted, and this means of course a great decrease in value ; land at Standon, Essex, house and land at Godmanchester, the advowson of Stanground and a rent-charge there, and money to buy property in Cambridge.

He also induced Henry, Earl of Huntingdon, Sir Francis Hastings, Sir Francis Walsingham, Sir Wolfstan and Lady Mary Dixey, Dr. Alexander Nowell, Sir Henry Mildmay of Graces, and other men of wealth and position, especially in London, to bestow gifts on the college, which then became able to maintain fourteen Fellows and fifty Scholars.

The Statutes of the college were signed 10 October, 1585, and are preserved at the college. There is a contemporary copy of these Statutes at Dogmersfield, showing that they were signed by Sir Walter, and as witnesses by Anthon. Mildmaye,

Hum. Mildmaye (Sir Walter's two sons), Joh. Hammon, Thom. Byng, W. Lewin, Tim. Bright, and Edw. Downing.

Among other interesting documents at the college is a Deed of Mortmain of the time of Cromwell, which carries a grand seal in splendid condition that displays quite clearly the Long Parliament in Session.

In the Statutes Sir Walter wrote :—" I wish all to understand that the one object I set before me in erecting this College was to render as many as possible fit for the administration of the Divine Word and Sacraments."

He never meant, however, that his college should be a School of Divinity and nothing more, for he applied to Queen Elizabeth for licence to found "an Everlasting College of Sacred Theology, Science, Philosophy, and the High Arts."

The founder's pious intentions were not always regarded, for there are early complaints of the services at Emmanuel College Chapel, the students lolling on forms and pledging each other in bumpers at the Sacrament. In a report to Archbishop Laud is said :—" In Emmanuel College their Chapel is not consecrate. Before Prayers begin the Boyes come in and sitt downe and putt on, and talk aloude of what they list."

When Sir Walter visited the college at the dedication festival in 1587, the Mayor and Corporation of Cambridge presented him with a gift, costing 45s. 11d., and in the accounts of the Corporation there are entries of 23s. and 55s. respectively for presentations to Sir Walter on the occasions of two visits to Cambridge.

Laurence Chaderton was the first Master of the college, and so continued till 1622, when he resigned.

The college is in the form of a double quadrangle, being of the same design as that adopted by Sir Walter for his house at Apethorpe. The range on the south side of the front court was the only entirely new building erected by Sir Walter. The chapel (now the Library), the hall, the kitchen, and the buildings on the west side of the main court were adapted to college purposes from the ancient buildings left by the Black Friars.

Sir Walter's building was not very substantial, and was pulled down in 1720, being replaced by a range of buildings that was burnt down in 1811 and rebuilt to the same design.

Sir Walter was so much of a Puritan that he made the chapel (now the Library) stand N. and S. instead of E. and W. This was not pleasing to Queen Elizabeth, who, on completion of the building, said to him when he came to Court:—"Sir Walter, I hear you have erected a puritan foundation." "No, Madam," replied he, "far be it from me to countenance anything contrary to your established laws, but I have set an acorn, which when it comes to be an oak, God alone knows what will be the fruit of it." The present chapel stands E. and W.

EMMANUEL COLLEGE, CAMBRIDGE. MILDMAY WING ON THE RIGHT

Queen Elizabeth, nevertheless, was a benefactress to the college by bestowing on it a rent-charge of £16 13s. 4d. taken from a gift of hers to Oxford. Grace Lady Mildmay, and Sir Henry, grandson to Sir Walter, were also contributors, as was Thomas Mildmay, for a silver can he presented was stolen from the college in 1684.

In connection with this college it is interesting to note that John Harvard, founder of the celebrated Havard College, Cambridge, America, was educated at Emmanuel College, and consequently at the tercentenary festival of that college on the 19th June, 1884, Harvard was represented by Charles Eliot Norton, M.A., Professor there of the History of Art.

Sir Henry St. John-Mildmay also attended the festival as representative of the Founder's family.

The arms of Emmanuel College are the Mildmay lion holding a green wreath, and Emmanuel on a scroll.

Sir Walter was author of *A Note to Knowe a Good Man*, and Latin poems, but both are lost.

Danbury, in Essex, was purchased by Sir Walter from the Earl of Northampton in the reign of Edward VI, and he is said to have built the house there in which his younger son lived.

There was an exchange of lands in 1551 between King Edward VI, the Princess Elizabeth, and Sir Walter Mildmay, when the last surrendered lands in Wiltshire and Essex, and acquired lands in Oxfordshire, and the manor and park of Apethorpe, anciently Apelthorpe, in Northamptonshire, that once belonged to Lord Mountjoy.

The house at Apethorpe, with double quad-rangles, was begun by Sir Walter about the year 1564, presumably on the site of an old manor-house belonging in the reign of King Henry VI to a family named Keble, and an old chimneypiece found in an outbuilding was pronounced by archi-tects to be of that period. Sir Walter's son, Sir Anthony, considerably enlarged the house, and Sir Francis Fane added windows and gables to the front in 1723.

Sir Walter placed his arms and those of his wife over the north gateway leading to the court, also over the chimneypiece in the dining-room with his motto "*Virtute non vi*," and initials W. M.

About the same time the manor of Sheviock, Cornwall, was granted to him, and sold by him to Thomas Carew in 1558.

The manor of Little Weldon in Northampton-shire was passed to Sir Walter in the fifth year of Edward VI, and this manor he exchanged for lands in Somerset.

"Patent Roll 933. 5 & 6 Philip & Mary. Pt. 1. Membr. 18.

"In consideration of the manor of Little Weldon, Co Northants granted the King and Queen by Sir Walter Mildmay knt, and for the sum of £745 6 5½ paid by the said Sir Walter and by Henry Coddenham gent: the King and Queen grant to the said Sir Walter Mildmay knt, and the said Henry Coddenham, all their Lordship and manor of Queen's Camel otherwise called East Camel, and the advowson of the Vicarage and Church, in the County of Somerset parcel of the lands called Richmond lands, and also all that meadow there, Home Close, and the lately disparked Park there called Camel Park containing by estimation 120 acres, and all their messuages, lands &c in the hamlets of Hazlegrove, Parvell, and Langleigh and the meadow Langleigh in the Co : Somerset, with all granges, mills, houses, watercourses &c, courtsleet, view of frankpledge, waifs and strays, &c, fairs, markets, tolls, customs, franchises, priveleges, profits &c in East Camel and Hazlegrove, Parvell and Langleigh all being parcel of Richmond lands, as fully, freely, and wholly as they were held and enjoyed by any Earl or Countess of Richmond, or by any Duke of Richmond, or by William late Earl of Southampton. They further grant all woods, underwoods, and trees growing upon the premises within the soil thereof. All which premises thus given and granted are valued at the clear yearly value of £67 5 8. To have and to hold to the said Sir Walter and Henry and the heirs of Walter of the Crown in Chief by the service of one fortieth part of one knight's fee.

" Dated at Westminster 18th day of July."

The above copy of the Patent in the Record Office, interesting in itself, is given because county historians do not seem able to decide where Little Weldon was situate. We have seen stated the counties of Norfolk, Suffolk, and Essex besides the correct one of Northamptonshire. Little Weldon is near Corby in that county.

In August, 1571, Queen Elizabeth granted lands to Sir Walter in the forest of Rockingham, and other grants he received for his services, some of which he exchanged.

He was returned to Parliament in 1553 as Member for Maldon, Essex, and from 1556 to the year of his death represented the county of Northampton.

It is recorded of him that he was the first to make a speech of two hours' duration, and that it was a wise and honest speech. He was an eloquent speaker with the great gift of a melodious voice.

Cecil, Lord Burghley, writing from Reading, 26 September, 1570, says :—"Sir Walter Mildmay and I are sent to the Scottish Queen—God be our guide for neither of us like the message." They were sent to Mary with proposals from Queen Elizabeth and their joint letter to their sovereign describes their first interviews.

"It may please Your Most Excellent Majestie although we have no matter of much importance to write of concerning our charge yet we knowing it our dutie to notifie our beginning and Your Majestie's expectation to understand the same, we are bold to trouble Your Majestie with this our letter for discharge of the same.

" We could not before this daye being Sundaye in the afternoone well come to this house, the wayes being so harde to passe with anie speede. And being come hither about three of the clocke, we, after some pause, repaired to this Queene of Scots, beinge in her side chamber where shee was under her Clothe of Estate. And, at our entrie shee came towards us and after our reverences done and Your Majestie's letters delivered to her, shee saide there could be nothing on earth more welcome than to have anie person sente to her by Your Majestie, her gude sister, after that shee hath beene so longe tyme here in your Realme without anie comfort, and alsoe to receive letters from Your Majestie which shee had not nowe of longe tyme done. And so shee opened Your Majestie's letters and in reading of them wee perceived that shee changed her countenance, as seeming to be much troubled thereby, which alsoe shee immediately expressed by her wordes, for shee saide, as shee was alwayes glad to heare from Your Majestie, and as shee was comforted with oure cominge, so was shee now muche grieved to perceive that her gude will and minde to please Your Majestie was not so understood and nothinge more grieved her than to be noted by Your Majestie withe the cryme of ingratitude which wordes she expressed withe a sorrowful sound and a watery eye, and then shee saide that, as shee had alwayes offered to Your Majestie to do anie thinge that withe reason and honor shee mighte to serve Your

Majestie's pleasure, so shee was still readie to perform such thinges, with manie faire wordes. And then wee told her that Your Majestie in hope thereof had sent us twoe her and so brieflie wee uttered the cause of oure cominge according to the wordes contained in our Commission and all this beinge spoken by her and us in suche sort as wee thinke others standing bye heard not. Shee then lifted up her speeche somewhat higher and saide shee never did offend Your Majestie in any speeche, hereof shee would be reported by anie that ever was in her companie, and for her thoughtes shee referred herself to Almightie God his Judgment and wished her harte and thoughtes mighte bee open to Your Majestie with sundrie other vehement speeches to that purpose. Whereupon wee were bolde to replie and saide that though God had not ordered that the harte of creatures shoulde be opened to express the inward thoughtes, yet the actes did alwayes discover and laye open the harte and therefore wee were sure Your Majestie had good proofes by manie her sundrie former actes to thinke shee had dealte unkindlie yea injuriouslie with Your Majestie and evil recompensed for your kindnesse. And therefore wee thoughte her best waye in that shee had heretofore so often tymes expressed and now to us declared, that shee woulde doe anie thinge to make satisfaction for the same to Your Majestie which you woulde no wyse seeke but with conditions honorable, favorable, and reasonable, and the cause of

the delay hitherto to treate hereof had onely proceeded from herself and such as have their evill
doinges under her authoritie. And soe, with some
further wordes of lyke sorte wee made it manifest
as well to herself as to others standinge bye that
shee was not to be taken so hard as by her wordes
shee would pretend, adding that at her leisure and
in a more convenient place wee woulde bee more
bolde with her if shee woulde soe permit or otherwise not to laye suche thinges before her as shee
woulde well perceive that Your Majestie had just
cause to charge her with both injurie and unkind-
nesse. Then shee altered her speeche and saide
shee woulde in anythinge to be required of her
doe her utmost to make amendes and woulde alsoe
soe answer us as shee trusted shee mighte, and
soe shee woulde make us to be judges of her con-
formitie. Shee did alsoe divers tymes declare the
desyre shee hath to see Your Majestie, whereuntoe
we answered that shee ought to consider that
princes be like mountaines that can hardlie meete,
such is their condition that they lacke therein the
commoditie that private persons doe enjoy. And
so wee ended this present tyme saying wee would
not further trouble her, but that at her commoditie
the next daye wee would wayte on her, to com-
mune with her further, whereuntoe shee gladly
agreed, and willed us to make thereof anie hour,
but we referred that to herselfe. And so this
nighte shee hath appointed us to be withe her
about nyne in the morninge. Wee doe forbear to

sende this letter this nighte, to the ende that wee may alsoe herewith advertise Your Majestie what shall be done tomorrow.

"Oct 2.    This daye at nyne of the clocke in the forenoone, wee came to the Queene of Scots beinge in a private gallery where shee secluded her companie, and haveing onlie there with her My Lord of Shrewsbury, the Bishop of Ross and us twoe, shee saide shee coulde not but continue her greefe that shee conceived by Your Majestie's letters and before shee could enter into communication of any other matters, shee desyred us to heare what shee could saye in her defence, and alsoe what wee woulde charge her with, so that shee might answere. Whereuntoe wee told her that wee had no meaning to charge her with anie lyinge except by her defence of herselfe shee woulde occasion us to doe.   And in the end shee consented and entered into greate and earneste attestations of her conscience and how muche shee desyred Your Majestie's favour and how void shee was of evill thought, and then wee begonne to charge her withe all manner of [obliterated] contayned in oure instructions, beginninge withe her pretence made to Your Highness' title, and soe with all thinges unkindlie done in Scotland and persons lyinge here in England.   To all whiche shee laboured to give particular answeres but wee found her most troubled and amazed that wee charged her to have had intelligence with Your Majestie's enemies, wherein shee would not denye but shee understood divers thinges from them, but they never had anie comfort from her, and charginge her that shee did not well in concealinge of thinges uttered to her, shee saide when shee made so earnest suite at Bolton to come to see Your Majestie shee meant then to have shewed Your Majestie some thinges that she otherwise coulde not doe. In the debate of these thynges shee oftentymes fell intoe weepinge and sorrowfull speeches, and so wee continued by her owne occasions and repititions of her defence until 12 of the clocke.

"This morning unlookedfor wee have seene winter enter intoe these Peakyish mountaines haveing a large snow fallen arounde aboute us soe as if this weather follow as it hath begune wee shall wish ourselves awaye. And in the mean season wee beseeche God Almightie longe to preserve Your Majestie to his Honour and the weale of all your humble and true subjects.

"From Chatsworth House the 2 October 1570."

The terms brought by Lord Burghley and Sir Walter Mildmay, as set forth in Spotswood, were very rigorous and apparently sincere, but Mary soon became convinced of Queen Elizabeth's insincerity.

In another letter describing the visit to Chatsworth, Sir Walter dwells on Mary's fascinating manner and soft words, but puts all down to "Arts and Intrigues."

He was one of the judges on her trial at Fotheringham, which is close to Apethorpe, and is shown in the contemporary drawing of the trial of Queen

E

Mary in the Calthorpe MS., cf. *The Tragedy of Fotheringay*, by Hon. Mrs. Maxwell Scott.

He was also present at her execution, and probably his strong Puritan anti-Popish feelings made him indifferent to the tragic fate of an unlucky woman.

Sir Walter was one of those consulted about the marriage of Queen Elizabeth with the Duke of Anjou, and seems to have been rather in favour of it.

In April, 1580, he, with Lord Burghley, Robert, Earl of Leicester, Sir Francis Walsingham, and others, Lords of the Council, wrote to Archbishop Grindal on the occasion of an earthquake in Yorkshire, commending his form of prayer to be used in all the parish churches for the turning of God's wrath from us.

The earthquake, according to the histories of the time of Queen Elizabeth, does not seem to have been very alarming.

The account drawn up by Wm. Stanton for Lord Burleigh of the "order of diets" for various persons at Hertford Castle, where two good messes of meat, always according to the days, were allowed, and always on the fish days two dishes of fish, mentions Sir Walter, and says there were told off to attend on him two gentlemen and five or six yeomen.

The expense of such attendance was probably not inconsiderable, for in the household accounts of Richard Bertie and the Duchess of Suffolk, his wife, appears in September, 1562, "To two keepers of

Sir Walter Mildmayes' 12/-" This means about
£4 according to the present value of money.

It is curious to read how money was obtained in
the time of Sir Walter for State purposes, for one
of his first duties in the reign of Queen Elizabeth
was when he was commissioned with Robert, Lord
Dudley and others to treat and compound with all
such persons as held £40 a year in land and refused to take the order of Knighthood. This
seems to indicate that knights were as freely made
in the sixteenth century as in the twentieth.

Sir Walter also, and others, furnished lists of
persons to whom Privy Seals could be sent, or, in
other words, persons who could be made to contribute
to the Queen's needs, and were able to make loans.
A forced contribution somewhat contradicts his
remarks about the Queen made in a speech
mentioned further on.

In 1588 he provided 5 lances, 15 light horse, and
8 petronels for the Queen's service.

From what is recorded of Sir Walter it is to be
gathered that he was a prudent, high-minded man,
unbending in public matters, but gentle in private
life, and anxious to do good in all ways.

He served his sovereign and his country faithfully and well, and was, as Camden says, a man
who " for his virtue, wisdom, and piety, favour to
learning and learned men, hath worthily deserved
to be registered among the best men of his age."
And again:—" One who discharged the offices of a
good citizen and a good man."

A contemporary account says :—" The Prince and Council made great accounts of his wisdom, in Council or in Star Chamber his onely word passed as law, to all suitors he was a comfort, most modest in speech and behaviour.    He spake words before his death of great moment, yea, his gracious and last adieu is worthy to be in letters of gold."

Unfortunately his last adieu has not been preserved.

His daughter-in-law, wife of Sir Anthony, records in her diary :—" Myne owne observation of Sir Walter Mildemay.    Having beene with him almost twenty years uprysing and downe lying in his house, who was so wyse, eloquent, and method-icall in all his speeches which proceeded from a clere judgment and true grounded discernment of whatever he spake of with the applause of all men that heard him."

Miss Aikin writes of him as:—" One of the most irreproachable public characters, and best patriots of his age."

Fuller, in his quaint way, thus expresses Sir Walter's conduct and its consequences :—" Being employed by virtue of his office to advance the Queen's treasure, he did it industrially, faithfully, conscionably, without wronging the subject, being very tender of their priveleges, insomuch that he once complained in Parliament, that many subsidies were granted, but no grievances redressed, which words being misrepresented to the Queen made her to disaffect him, setting in a Court cloud but

SIR WALTER MILDMAY, CHANCELLOR OF THE EXCHEQUER TO
QUEEN ELIZABETH

in the sunshine of his Country and a clear conscience."

Writing from Apethorpe in September, 1569, to Cecil, Sir Walter says :—"that the Queen's safety and the preservation of the cause of religion, are the two pillars on which the security of the State is founded"; and in Parliament, in 1581, he eulogised the Queen. He spoke of the moderation of her Government and the prosperity which England had enjoyed while the rest of Europe was in flames. He dwelt on the successive attempts that had been made to destroy the Queen, and said that so far she had been able to encounter these plots at her own cost. The country had been called on for little or no assistance. The few subsidies for which she had asked had not covered half her expenses, and without loan or benevolences she had carried on the Government out of her private revenues. England under her moderate rule enjoyed more freedom than any nation under the sun. She had been personally a virtuous princess, unspotted in word or deed, merciful, temperate, a maintainer of peace and justice.

Edmund Bohun, in his *Character of Queen Elizabeth*, ed. 1693, says :—"She raised Sadler from nothing, Mildmay and Fortescue from mean fortunes to the honour of knighthood, and made them Privy Councillors for their good services, and lest that dignity should suffer by the meanness of their Estates, she gave them a competency, by way of addition to what they had before." The knighthood is wrong, for Sir Walter was knighted by King Edward VI.

Queen Elizabeth may well have been aware of Sir Walter's devotion to her, for she is said to have shown great grief at his death, on the 31st May, 1589. His will is dated 6 April, 1588 ; one bequest in it leaves to Lord Burleigh "a guilte potte with cover which the late Earle of Essex gave me." This has disappeared.

There are portraits of Sir Walter at Dogmersfield, one at Knole, and a threequarter-length on panel in black suit and hat with ruff, inscribed "A.D. 1573, ætat. suæ 52," belonging to W. R. Fane, Esq., of Fulbeck, which was purchased at the Apethorpe sale. There are also pictures of Sir Walter and his wife at Emmanuel College, fully described in the college magazine, Easter term, 1906, two of these pictures being accounted for in the following letter :—

"To the Rev. Dr. Richardson, Master of Emmanuel.

"ADMIRALTY, *April* 13, 1771.

"Sir, I have now in my possession the picture of your foundress Lady Mildmay, which is framed and is a proper companion to that of her husband which you was so obliging as to allow a place to in your College. You will receive this in the course of next week, and as I fear it is now the custom of mankind to have some advantage in everything they do, I shall hope for so hospitable and agreeable a dinner in the Lodge at Emmanuel College some time next summer, as I met with when you was in possession only of Lady Mildmay's better half.

"I am with great regard
"Your most obedient humble Servant
"SANDWICH."

According to Grainger, the picture of Sir Walter mentioned in the preceding letter was given to the Earl of Sandwich by the Rev. H. Jerome de Salis, and said to be a portrait from life.

Curiously enough there is nothing in the records of Emmanuel College which enables the authorities there to identify the two pictures given by the Earl of Sandwich, but what is still more strange, the picture in the place of honour in the hall, and called the Founder's portrait, is almost certainly not a portrait of Sir Walter, for it bears no resemblance to any of the other portraits of him, which do all resemble each other.

It was purchased at a sale in Norfolk, and the catalogue of that sale makes no mention of a picture of Sir Walter, but does mention that of a Dutch burgomaster, which this so-called Founder's picture seems to represent. There is a replica of this picture at Dogmersfield.

On the 7th June, 1907, there was sold at Christie's a picture belonging to the Duke of Fife, called Sir Walter Mildmay, by Kyston, a painter not mentioned by either Bryan, Pilkington, or

Redgrave. The picture is a half-length 37″ × 28½″, and represents a grey-haired man with a slight resemblance to undoubted likenesses of Sir Walter; but by his side are a sword and helmet, things not compatible with Sir Walter's career. In one corner is a coat of arms, correct, and the motto " Allah Ta Harah," of which Sir Walter had never heard.

In May, 1911, Captain Charles St. John-Mildmay of Hollam wrote to us to say he had just bought a half-length portrait on panel of Sir Walter Mildmay.

Sir Walter's signature is to be seen on many documents, among those at Dogmersfield being the copy of the Statutes of Emmanuel College before referred to, and an order for the payment of 6s. 8d. to Iveson, a Queen's messenger.

Sir Walter had a house in the cloisters of St. Bartholomew, for which he paid the peppercorn rent of 4d. a year, and there he probably died, for he was buried in St. Bartholomew Church, and his monument there of rich coloured marbles and alabaster is of course well known.

The inscription is simple, and records :—

" Here lies Sir Walter Mildmay, Knight, and Mary his wife

" He died on the last day of May 1589

" She on the 16th March 1576

" They left 2 sons and 3 daughters

" He founded Emmanuel College, Cambridge

" He died Chancellor and under Treasurer of the Exchequer

" And a Member of Her Majesty's Privy Council."

There are seven shields on the tomb :—
Mildmay—Mildmay and Walsingham—Barrett
and Mildmay—Mildmay and Capel—Brouncker
and Mildmay—Leveson and Mildmay—Mildmay
and Sherrington.

As long ago as May, 1785, a writer in the
*Gentleman's Magazine* drew attention to the
ruinous condition of Sir Walter's monument, and
suggested that Emmanuel College should repair
damages. This apparently the College did not do,
for when the monument was moved from the arch
opposite to the tomb of Revere to its present
situation in 1865, it had fallen into a terrible state
of dilapidation ; but in 1870, at the instigation of
the present writer, was by direction of the late
Mr. Bingham St. John-Mildmay admirably and
accurately restored at considerable expense.

Others of the family were buried in Sir Walter's
vault, one being his great granddaughter, Rachel
Bromley.

There was a MS. of Sir Walter's at Apethorpe,
consisting of a series of sentences giving good
advice to his son Anthony. This, by permission
of Anthony Mildmay, thirteenth Earl of Westmoreland, was copied by the late Rev. Arundel
St. John-Mildmay and printed. In it the Chancellor says : "Speak well of all, speak ill of none."
"Choose thy wife by virtue only, seke no match
above thy degree." "Thy children bring up in
virtue and learning." "At thy table be honestly
merry, but nothing pass thee to the hurt of any

present or absent." "Grieve not thy tenants with
exactions "—and many more wise admonitions of
a like kind—ending with, "Finally, my son, Love
God, Fear him, Learn to live and die."

Sir Walter married, 25 May, 1546, Mary,
sister of Sir Francis Walsingham, Secretary of
State, a stiff, stern woman and a hard and rigid
Puritan.

Sir Francis was at one time Ambassador in
France, and complains to his brother-in-law in his
letters that his allowance was quite insufficient for
his expenses, so Sir Walter helped to pay for his
journey when returning home.

At Fulbeck are two volumes of Cicero purchased
at the Apethorpe sale, given by Sir Francis Walsingham to Sir Walter Mildmay in the last year of
the reign of Queen Mary, with the inscription :—

"Quo me mea fata trahunt, nescio."

Sir Walter's daughter Martha married 16 January,
1568–9, Sir William Brouncker, ancestor to Lord
Brouncker ; Winifred married William Fitz-
William of Gainspark, Essex, an ancestor of
Earl FitzWilliam ; and Christian (or Catherine)
married, first, Charles Barrett of Belhus, Essex,
ancestor to Lord Dacre, and became mother of
Lord Barrett of Newburgh, and secondly Sir John
Leveson.

# SIR ANTHONY MILDMAY

SIR WALTER MILDMAY'S elder son Anthony succeeded to the Apethorpe estate and others, and bought Nassington Manor, near Apethorpe. Anthony was educated at the Peter House, Cambridge, and according to Nicholls, in the *Progresses of Queen Elizabeth*, it is to him that reference is made in the account of the reception of the Queen at Cambridge in August, 1564, in which is said :—" She went into Pembroke Hall and Peter House, and in both places heard an oration, and at the Peter House she much commended the son of Sir Walter Mildmay, who, being a child, made a very neat and trim oration, and pronounced it very aptly and distinctly."

Anthony, when quite young, married, in 1567, Grace Sherrington, a Wiltshire lady, a woman of considerable ability, and who brought him a large fortune. This marriage was arranged for her before she was fifteen, and took place in her sixteenth or seventeenth year, for she was born in 1551. Grace, according to her diary, had great difficulties to contend against over the inheritance left her by her father, Sir Henry Sherrington of Lacock Abbey, Co. Wilts, and says that her sisters and uncle intrigued against her.  Most probably there was a temporary misunderstanding, for though she did not inherit Lacock Abbey, she was left a great deal of land in and adjoining the parish of Lacock, viz. Bewley Court, Bowden Park, and manors of Queenfield and Sheen, all of which were sold by her grandson, Mildmay Fane, Earl of Westmoreland.

Anthony does not seem to have developed such intellectual powers as those of his father, but he became a man of importance in his county and at Court.

At least once he went into action, when he with Sir Edward Montagu moved with their men and horses against the rebels at Newton Field.  Sir Henry Mildmay commanded their horsemen and behaved very gallantly.

Anthony was fond of travel, and was almost certainly employed by Queen Elizabeth in various capacities, but his first great public duty came when he was nominated by her Ambassador to King Henry IV of France in 1596, on which occasion he was knighted.  Writing to thank for the appointment, he professed to be unsuited for the post from his want of knowledge of the country and language, as he had not been there for twenty-one years.

Sir Anthony, soon after reaching Paris, made an offer from the Queen to the King for the recovery of Calais, on the condition that it might remain in her hands until the money expended had been repaid. The King, asking who should command the army, and Sir Anthony answering the Earl in chief and Sir John Norreys as second, with a disdainful smile, is said to have replied :— " Que le Général Norreys avait trop de besogne taillée en Irlande, et que sa Majesté ne laisseroit jamais son cousin d'Essex elloigner de son costillon." Upon the Ambassador's report of this remark, Her Majesty returned four lines in her own hand, upon receipt of which from Sir Anthony's hands the King, having read them with a manifest alteration of countenance, was ready, lifting up his arm, to have stricken him, but checking himself, commanded him to leave the chamber.

Queen Elizabeth's little note would be interesting reading, and probably startling, for she was apt to put plainly what she had to say.

According to Fuller, Sir Anthony visited Geneva during the time he was Ambassador, which hardly seems likely.

Opinions certainly differed as to Sir Anthony's judgment concerning affairs in France, for Lord Burghley, writing to his son, 8 July, 1597, says :— " Your other letter from Sir Anthony Mildmay with the copy of the King's letter to him, can scantly have any good scence whereon to found any present counsell. For I see no likelihood for the French King to seke peace at this present."

Dudley Carleton, in a letter of 6 June, 1598, writes :—" I find Sir Anthony Mildmay is not to be employed again, his assurance that the peace would

never come to pass has discredited his judgment."
These two statements are contradictory, for Lord
Burghley credits Sir Anthony with but little sense
for saying there would be peace in France, and
Carleton says he is condemned for affirming there
would not be peace.

Chamberlain did not rate him over highly, for in
one of his letters to Carleton he writes :—" I am
exceeding glad to heare how well you are entertained by my Lord Ambassador of whom I presumed no lesse, for though I always knew him to
be *pancorum hominum* yet he hath ever shewed himself an honorable fast friend where he found vertue
and desert."

Sir Anthony was not *persona grata* to Henry IV,
who disliked his cold, uncordial manner, but Sir
Anthony did not reciprocate the ill-feeling, for in
his observations on the State of France during his
Embassy, written in August, 1597, he begins :—
" The King is a man of very good and tractable
nature."

In a folio " History of England by several
Hands " is said that, in 1597, " Queen Elizabeth
remonstrated with Henry IV of France, and that
her statement was warmly expostulated with the
King by Sir Anthony Mildmay Her Majesty's
Residentiary.  He was indeed a gentleman of a
true honest English principle, and would now and
then take the freedom to charge the French King's
Council with Trickery and Legerdemain, and used
to say that they made a property of the English

by shifting them off with trifling, loose, and ambiguous Answers."

Notwithstanding what Carleton says, Sir Anthony was again offered the post of Ambassador in France in 1598, which he declined, and his reasons for declining may very probably be found in a letter of his to Sir Robert Cecil, in which he sets forth that he has served the Queen both in Court and other places for thirty years at great charge, wherein he has consumed whatever his father left it in his power to sell. Has lately bestowed his daughter in marriage, parting with £300 in land for her advancement ; his debts are great through his last employment, and what remains is but a bare rent, which disables him almost utterly from keeping open his doors any longer, and what grieves him most disfurnishes him from doing Her Majesty service. He prays Cecil to make this known to the Queen that his absence from attending her may not be mistaken, and the want known may be either supplied by her bounty or his default pardoned. If the Queen does not think him worthy of any reward for his long services, prays for leave to absent himself for three years beyond the seas, to recover strength of body, mind, and means.[1]

The dating of this letter is interesting as showing that when in London he probably lived in the same house that his father had occupied.

Bohun, in his *Character of Queen Elizabeth*,

[1] Dated St. Bartholomew's, 26 October, 1599.

˙says :—" She would always remember to reward those who served her faithfully in foreign Courts," so let us hope Sir Anthony had a favourable answer to his letter.

Another letter of his to Cecil gives a glimpse of what was considered right in those days, for in it he deliberately offers Cecil a bribe of £100 to intervene on his behalf about the game on a chace.

Sir Anthony, writing in February, 1598–9, says :—" Fortune has cast me after all my travels on a country life " ; and he settled down at Apethorpe, where he entertained as magnificently as his means permitted, Lady Mildmay superintending everything.

One of the first mentions of his entertaining is when the Earl of Rutland and suite visited him, and Scriven, in his account of the Rutland family, enters 12 September, 1599 :—" Then at Sir Mildemays to the officers there xls."

A tract printed in 1603, the year of the progress of King James I from Scotland, tells us that the monarch when passing from Burleigh House to Hinchingbrook dined at Apethorpe, and that there :—" The tables were newly covered with costly banquets wherein everything that was most delititious for taste proved more delicate by the Arte that made it seeme beauteous to the eye : the Ladye of the house being one of the most excellent confectioners in England, though I confesse many honourable women very expert."

After the dinner, Sir Anthony presented to King

James a Barbary horse and a very rich saddle with furniture suitable thereto. There is also a record of Sir Anthony sending two bucks to Belvoir in 1612 for the entertainment there of the King.

Grace Lady Mildmay's household books have been preserved. They are in her own handwriting, and a specimen of expenditure is given for the week ending 24 June, 1593.

| | | | |
|---|---|---|---|
| Bread fine | 9 dozen and 1 | Bread coarse | 29 dozen |
| Beer | 8 hogsheads | Beef | 41 pieces |
| Mutton | 66 joints | Veal | 6 joints |
| Tongues | 51 | Pigs | 4 |
| Capons | 7 | Lambs | 1 |
| Herons | 2 | Ducks | 29 |
| Chickens | 33 | Pigeons | 29 |
| Rabbits | 2 | Pickerell | 11 |
| Breams | 3 | Tench | 4 |
| Perches | 6 | Ling | 1 |
| Hartechokes | 15 | Haberdius (large cod) | 9 |
| Brewetts | 1 sticke | Roasting Yealls | 2 |
| Pasties | 3 | Pies | 2 |
| Custards | 2 | Tarts | 2 |
| Candles | 7 lbs | Butter fresh | 34 lbs |
| Coals | 35 bushels | Butter salt | 6 lbs |
| Rotches | 6 (wild ducks) | | |

Decidedly a meat diet, for vegetables are not mentioned, except perhaps as "Hartechokes," very little given in the way of sweets, and what perhaps is more remarkable, no milk or cheese. What "Roasting Yealls" and "Brewetts 1 sticke" represent we have not been able to discover.

Professor Thorold Rogers, in his *History of Prices*, when writing of this period, says :—"Onions, nettles, leeks, and pears were the only esculent

F

vegetables. We probably also possessed cabbage, but I have never found either seed or plants quoted."

According to Madame Duchaux, in her book, *The Fields of France*, there were at this same time in that country Brussels sprouts, three other kinds of cabbage, winter greens, spinach, sorrel, beetroot, turnips, carrots, beans, peas, lettuce, sweet basil, all kinds of herbs, cucumbers, garlic, onions, leeks, rhubarb, and fennel. It certainly seems strange that such a traveller as Sir Anthony, who must have experienced the advantages of so many vege-tables, should not have thought of bringing some back and establishing them at home.

In July, 1598, there is an entry of 5s. for tobacco pipes. Surely one of the earliest mentions of such a purchase.

Again, travelling expenses for forty-three people and thirty-four horses from Apethorpe to London, and there not being any item of expenditure for lodgings would seem to indicate that the company slept in the conveyances in which they travelled.

|  | £ | s. | d. |
|---|---|---|---|
| Suppers . . . | 3 | 7 | 11 |
| Breakfasts . . | 2 | 5 | 4 |
| Rewards . . . | | 8 | 2 |
| Horse meat . . | 3 | 2 | 10 |
| Smith and Sadler . | | 12 | 11 |
| Total . . | 9 | 17 | 2 |

Lady Rose Weigall, *née* Fane, in an account she drew up of Grace Lady Mildmay writes :—

" The Monasteries, the chief centres of charity, being abolished, the care of the sick and poor in country districts fell naturally upon those who had acquired Church lands.

" Queen Elizabeth's first poor law had been passed, and the first workhouse established, but the poverty and misery continued very great. Grace Lady Mildmay threw her whole energies into the work of relieving distress. One of the greatest troubles was the almost total absence of provision for medical help, and she set to work to study medicine thoroughly, the result being several volumes of elaborate prescriptions and recommendations, one volume being labelled 'for use in the workhouse.'

" Her daughter, who classified all these recipes, added a quaint preface, in which she says :—'Certain brief Collections and observations concerning man's body drugs, preparations of medecines, and signs of disease left in writing by that Reverend Ladie, the Ladie Mildmay, who spent a great part of her days in the search and practice thereof, and left this troublesome world wherein she conversed so much continually with Mortality for that of perpetual rest and Immortality in the year 1620.'

" The collections are curious and pathetic in their strange simplicity, and, needless to say, there is no trace of science. The drugs, nearly all herbs, are employed in much the same proportions as they are now, and very great reliance is placed on 'Quilts,' i.e. poultices and fomentations, for all of which elaborate directions are given. The only notion of preventive medicine was apparently periodical dosings. Children especially seemed to have been drenched with oceans of physic, but the hints on their ordinary diet give one the idea that this probably prevented their death from over-eating and heavy food.

" It is difficult to realise that to this excellent, care-ful mother, and housekeeper, such things as tea, coffee, sugar, potatoes and most of our common vegetables were either unknown, or known only as costly dainties quite unattainable in ordinary life, that a nursery lived chiefly on beer and meat, and that the medicine of a child ' 3 years old suffering with its teeth' is recommended to be given at night in its posset of beer.

"Charity organisation was another feature of Lady Grace's work. She anticipated some of the modern systems in the directions she wrote out for the charities in her different parishes. No able-bodied person was to be relieved except through work, and when families had got into difficulties a carefully planned system of loans and small bonuses was laid down. Charities were maintained for apprenticing poor children yearly to various trades. (These latter charities are still in existence.) Clothing was to be given to poor widows in the shape of petticoats of green baize, at that time a highly valued material, and it is said that the old women of the district cherish green petticoats to this day.

" These varied charities were made possible by a

careful administration of her expenditure, and her house books show that no waste was allowed and everything carefully calculated."

The above account gives an admirable description of a judicious Lady Bountiful of the period, but we would take exception to the statement that sugar was almost unknown to Lady Mildmay, for imported sugar had been in use in England for more than two centuries before her time, and though perhaps not within the means of the poor, could certainly be procured by anyone so well off as Lady Mildmay, and the possession of it no doubt enabled the writer of the tract of 1603 to describe her as "one of the most excellent confectioners in England."

When Grace Lady Mildmay's picture was at Apethorpe she was said to step out of it at night, pass through the house and village to see that all was in order, and scatter silver pennies for the needy. Though the picture is now gone, perhaps her ghost haunts the place she tended so wisely and so well.

James I was so pleased with a visit to Apethorpe in 1603 that he repeated it more than once, and on one occasion first met there Villiers, afterwards Duke of Buckingham. In accordance with his usual custom he presented a statue of himself. It is of stone, and used to stand in a niche on the south front of the court ; but when this was pulled down in 1742 it was removed and is now in the front hall.

Sir Anthony and his wife were buried in

Apethorpe Church under an altar tomb of black and white marble on which are the recumbent figures of Sir Anthony and his Lady. He is in armour, in the posture of prayer, his head on a pillow, having a handsome but weak face; she at his left side, in the same posture, richly dressed in an ornamental robe, large ruff, and jewelled girdle, her face showing intellectual power. On the canopy over them is inscribed "Just, Wise, Devout, Charitable." By the side of the tomb figures of Justice, Wisdom, Charity pouring wine into a chalice, and Devotion resting her right arm on a pillar. On the upper part of the east end a Virgin in folding robes, having in her right hand a cross, in her left a tablet. At the west end Hope raising her eyes to heaven, her right hand on her breast, her left leaning on an anchor. At the centre over all a female figure with an infant.

On the monument is the following interesting inscription :—"Here sleepeth in the Lord with a certaine hope of Resurrection Sir Anthony Mildmay, Knight, eldest sonne of Sir Walter Mildmay, Knight, Chancellor of the Exchequer to Queen Elizabeth. He was Ambassador from Queen Elizabeth to the Most Christian King of France Henry IV, A.D. 1596. He was to Prince and Countrie faithfull and serviceable in Peace and Warre, to Friends constant, to Enemies reconcileable, bountiful and loved Hospitality.

He died September 11, 1617.
Here also lyeth Grace Lady Mildmay the only wife

TOMB OF SIR ANTHONY AND GRACE LADY MILDMAY IN APETHORPE CHURCH

of the said Sir Anthony Mildmay, one of the heiresses of Sir Henry Sherrington, of Lacock, in the County of Wilts, who lived fifty years married to him, and three years a widow after him. She was most devout, unspotedly chaste Mayd, Wife, and Widow, compassionate in Heart, and charitably helpful with Physick, Cloathes, Nourishment, or Counsel to any in Misery. She was most careful and wise in managing worldly estate so as her life was a blessing to hers, and in her death she blessed them, which happened

July 27, 1620.

Thus this worthy pair having lived here worthily, dyed comfortably, beloved of God, lamented of men, to whose memory and to incite to the example of their virtues, Sir Francis Fane, Knight, son and heir to the R^t Honb^le Mary Lady Le Despencer, and his wife Mary, daughter and heir to the said Sir Anthony and Ladie Mildmay have erected this monument.

A.D. 1621."

The last part of this inscription does not seem to agree closely with the terms of the will of Sir Anthony Mildmay, for in that will he leaves everything to his wife Grace, and desires her to spend £1000 on his tomb in Apethorpe Church.

Mary, the only child of Sir Anthony and Grace Lady Mildmay, was born in 1582, married in 1599, and died in 1640. It was through her marriage with Sir Francis Fane, first Earl of Westmoreland that the Apethorpe estate passed into the possession of the Fanes.  Sir Anthony in a document he left gives his reasons for cutting his brother Humphrey out of the entail, "Because he (his brother) would not make a proper provision for his wife though she brought him property.  That his daughter, his only child, was nearer and dearer to him than his brother.  That his brother had been well provided for by their father.  That his brother constantly quarrelled with him."  But there seems to have been another reason, for Grace Lady Mildmay says in her diary that Sir Anthony was obliged to cut off the entail to enable him to raise money to pay off his debts.

Apethorpe is built in two courts, one containing the principal apartments, the other the servants' quarters.  One court has been rather spoilt by part having been altered in 1742 to a classic style, which, though good classic, does not accord with Tudor architecture.

The fine chimneys are noticeable, and it has been asserted that they were copied from those at Lacock Abbey, but Mr. C. H. Talbot, the present owner of Lacock, assures us that this is an error, and that the chimneys of the two houses do not resemble each other.  Over the door of the tower is a shield with the arms of Sir Walter, and another with the arms of Sir Walter and his wife.  In the dining-room on one side of the chimneypiece are the arms of Sir Walter, his initials W. M., and his motto " Virtute non vi."  The date on this mantel-

GATEWAY, APETHORPE

piece is 1562. The inscription on the centre panel explains the motto of " Virtute non vi," and assures the reader that virtue makes us men, but force makes us beasts.

The interesting chimney from the dining-room fireplace is in that part of the house next to the garden, where remains of plain gables may be seen earlier and better than the curvilinear gables at the front.

The panelled gallery in the principal court is 111 ft. 8 in. long, 20 ft. 8 in. wide, and 14 ft. 6 in. high. The original panelled dining-hall or refectory, with a gallery, is now the servants' hall. Some of the principal rooms have chimneypieces and ceilings that date back to the period of Sir Walter or that of his son.

The earliest date on Apethorpe Hall is 1564, but on the church 1551, the year the property was acquired.

The Hon. Julian Fane, a gifted member of the Westmoreland family, who died in 1870, gives this poetical description of Apethorpe Hall :—

" The moss-grey mansion of my father stands
  Parked in an English pasturage as fair
As any that the grass-green Isle can show.
Above it rise deep-wooded lawns ; below
A brook runs riot through the pleasant lands,
And blabs its secret to the merry air.
The village peeps from out deep poplars, where
A grey bridge spans the stream, and all beyond
In sloping and sweet acclivities

The many-dimpled laughing landscape lies.
Four square, and double-courted, and grey-stoned
Two quaint quadrangles of deep latticed walls
Grass-grown, and moaned about by troops of doves
The ancient house !   Collegiate in name
As in its aspect, like the famous Halls
Whose hoary fronts make reverend the groves
Of Isis on the banks of classic Cam."

If the Hon. Julian Fane were yet alive he could not now write of his "father's mansion," for Apethorpe has passed by sale from the possession of the Fanes.

There is a portrait of Sir Anthony Mildmay at Emmanuel College, and there are portraits of him, his wife, and his daughter belonging to W. V. R. Fane, Esq., of Fulbeck, Co. Lincoln, that were purchased at the Apethorpe sale.   Those of Sir Anthony and his wife were originally fixed into the panelling at the end of the long gallery at Apethorpe.

The portrait of Sir Anthony is a full-length in black suit, with long, black leather boots and spur-straps, embroidered sword-belt; and helmet, breast-plate, gauntlets, and inlaid musquet in foreground. The inscriptions on it are :—"Patriæ causa et principis jussee in utrumque semper paratus fui. Anno ætatis suæ LXIII." On a scroll and on packets lying on the table :—"A Monsieur, Monsieur de Myldmay Ambassadeur de la royme d'Angle près du Roy." "For Her Majesty's special affaires." "To my honorable and loveinge Friend,

CHIMNEY-PIECE, APETHORPE, OF THE MILDMAY PERIOD

Sir Anthony Mildmaye, Knight, Her Ma^{ties} Ambassador resident withe the French Kynge.  Ro: Cecyll."

The last three inscriptions are evidently displayed for the purpose of commemorating Sir Anthony's important State duty.

An engraving of Sir Anthony differs in some of the accessories from the above picture, but absolutely agrees with the fine full-length of him at Emmanuel College.

Grace Lady Mildmay's portrait is a full-length in black dress.  The inscription on it is :—

> " The minde continualli imployed
> in good thinges avoideth evill,
> pleaseth God, and promiseth
> an happie end.
> An: Dom: 1613. ætatis suæ 62.

Also the end of the simples—a horned still—bagpipe still—is on the page of an open book, on which are depicted two retorts or stills, one evidently meant for the horned, and the other for the bagpipe.  This book is Lady Grace's " Book of Simples," or receipts, which still exists among the papers belonging to the Westmorland family.

The Apethorpe portrait of Mary Mildmay is also a full-length in black dress.  It is attributed to D. Mytens, Van Dyck's predecessor as Court painter.

Mr. Fane of Fulbeck owns a small vellum-bound copy of De Beza's *Pithie summe of the*

*Christian Faith* that has the initials G. M. on the outside, and at the end these lines:—

> " Seeke not to crave
>   that you would have
>   Then shall you finde
>   untoe your minde
>   That you like best
>   To give you rest.—" GRACE MILDEMAY."

Belonging to Christ's Hospital and hanging in the Board-room is an excellent small picture of Edward VI when Prince of Wales, said to have been painted by Holbein.

This picture, before it was done up a few years ago, bore an inscription stating that it was once the property of Sir Anthony Mildmay, Chamberlain to Queen Elizabeth. When presented to the hospital, or rather promised in 1837, for it was actually presented some years later, a letter came from a Mr. Shaw tracing the picture back to the possession of Sir Anthony.

We had thought that the title of Chamberlain came from ownership of Fingreth Manor that Sir Anthony's father bought, for the tenant of that manor had the honour of being Chamberlain to the Queen of England, of keeping her chamber and the door of the same on the day of her coronation, and of having for his fee the furniture of the chamber, basins, beds, etc., but Dr. Horace Round assures us that Fingreth passed to Humphrey, Sir Anthony's brother, so probably among the Court appointments held by Sir Anthony was at one time that of Chamberlain.

DANBURY PLACE, ESSEX

# SIR HUMPHREY MILDMAY OF DANBURY

HUMPHREY, Sir Walter's second son, was also educated at Cambridge.

He was Member for Higham Ferrers 1585–6, Sheriff of Essex 1593, and inherited the estates of Queen Camel, Somerset, and Danbury, Essex, with the adjacent property of Bycknacre Priory.

This Bycknacre was given by Henry VIII to Henry Polsted, who, in 1548, eleven years later, sold it to Sir Walter Mildmay, and of his grandson it was purchased by George Barrington of Little Baddow.

Humphrey married Mary Capel of Little Hadham, Herts, and a stone in Danbury Church records :—" Hoc lapide tegitur Humfredus | Mildmay Armiger patrenatus | Waltero Mildmay Saccarii | Cancellario et Consillario | Secretoris Admissionis R. Elizabethæ | Matre Maria Walsingham sorore | Francisci Walsingham eidem | Reginæ a Secretis Qui diu publice | utilis, domi Hospitalis, Sexagenarius | obiit nono Augusti, 1613."

The Rev. J. B. Plumtre, Rector of Danbury, has now placed (1906) a linoleum covering over the three

Mildmay slabs in the floor of Danbury Church to preserve them from further damage.

Humphrey was succeeded by his son Humphrey, born 1592, knighted 10 July, 1616, who married Jane, daughter of Sir John Crofts.

He was J.P. for Essex, High Sheriff of the county in 1636, and had to collect the ship-money, which, according to his letters and reports, he found a matter of extreme difficulty.

He also kept a diary extending from the year 1633 to 1666. The first part of this diary, which terminates at the 9th July, 1652, is at the British Museum, Harl. MS., No. 454. A copy of this part was sold by Sotheby and Wilkinson on the 10th July, 1857, for £5 5s., and is no doubt that now at Shoreham, Kent, having been purchased by Mr. Humphrey St. John-Mildmay of that place.

The diary shows that Humphrey had not in-herited any of the rigid puritanical characteristics of his grandfather and grandmother, for it is often in the style of the immortal Pepys, and contains numerous confessions of sins and expressions of regret.

It is on the whole a disappointing document, for references to public events are few and far between, and it is mainly a record of interminable lawsuits and incessant drinking bouts.

Some extracts are given :—

9 July, 1633. "Came Richard Rose a foot boye, that served M<sup>r</sup> John Lick, to serve me for wages, £4 per ann: and a cloake and suit as others have had."

A hideous record that appears occasionally.

SIR HUMPHREY MILDMAY OF DANBURY

20 July, 1633. "This morninge are seven hanged
at Tyburn for robberies."

He moves from Danbury on

1 November, 1633 :—"being Friday, I with my wife
and family came to London on a wett day, with
2 cartes, 6 men, 15 horses, besides the coach
horses."

More executions.

7 November, 1633 :—"the poor fryer Father Arthur
was hanged and quartered at Tyburne with a
world of lookers on."

1 December, 1633. "Jas Warde was hanged at Gray
Inn Lane Ende for rape."

Ladies received in their bedrooms.

5 March, 1634. "I wente to my Lady Avaldgravey
and satt with her a good time, who was then
in fisick and in bed."

4 May, 1634. "I wente to Lambeth and did swyme
at 7 of the clocke." A proof of how much
fresher and cleaner the Thames was then than
now. He refers occasionally to reading, and
mentions lending part of his Douai Bible to Mr.
Bourneby. Amongst the Ormonde papers is
" A note of bookes lefte by my sonne Humphrey
in Queen's Camel, Co. Somerset, since May 6,
1652." Twenty-five works are specified, including a Chaucer, a greate masse booke, one Bible
in English, Ben Jonson his workes, etc.

1 May, 1635. "We all went a Maying to Hyde
Park to see the Ladyes."

6 May, 1635. "At a play this day called the Moor of Venice."

7 May, 1635 :—"being the Holy Ascention of Our Lorde my sister Marye was married to M<sup>r</sup> Thomas Drucker, where I was all day with my two boys."

More horrors.

15 May, 1635. "I attended the Sessions at Newgate where 13 had judgment to be hanged, and Alex: Clarke to be burned."

He was not a faithful husband, for there are many entries like the following :—

3 November, 1635. "To M<sup>r</sup> Maine's to supper where I laughed and kissed the wenches exceedingly."

His brother Anthony was his constant companion in his revelries and even more dissipated. About this time and for the next few years he makes constant allusion to interviews with lawyers without stating exactly what the litigation was about. One of his legal advisers was his brother John.

12 December, 1635. "North hanged in Wood Street where he did his murther."

Showing that criminals were executed at the scene of their crime.

17 January, 1636, he was pricked for High Sheriff of Essex, and on the 26th agrees with George FitzJeffery to be his Under Sheriff, who is to pay £50 for his (Sir Humphrey's) use, £11 to the Judge's men, and find all his own expenses. In a letter to Sir Thomas

Puckering of 1636 there is :—" The Sheriff of
Essex lately did assess an hundred near him
at so much. Then he sent the high Constables to proportion it to the several towns
and persons which they did not do in the time
limited. He sends to them a second time,
and gives them so many days more, but they
were as neglectful as before. The High
Sheriff taking notice of their carelessness, he
forthwith gets half a dozen of waggons. With
these he goes in person to the houses of the
aforesaide High Constables and distrains their
goods which he causeth to be put in the
waggons. Then he sells them, so raiseth
that sum of money laid upon the whole
hundred." One can hardly imagine the plea-
sure-loving Sir Humphrey engaged in such a
business, so perhaps it was his deputy who
carried out the unpleasant transaction.

22 February, 1636, his son Edward died, as
　　recorded on a stone in Danbury Church, but
　　he does not mourn long, for on

17 March, 1636. "I wente to the great dinner of
　　M$^r$ Lathom, reader of the Middle Temple,
　　where was 100 great ones."
Other social events.

1 May, 1636. "Sir Arthur Capell hath slain in
　　Dewell Thomas Leventhorpe Baronett."
Sir Arthur was probably a cousin, Sir Hum-
phrey's mother having been Mary Capel.

G

2 May, 1636. "To my great expense attended my Lord Holland all day at Stratford in the duste."

At this time he was residing in the parish of St. John's, Clerkenwell, for his name is given on the 19th May as neglecting to pay his assessment in that parish for the relief of those infected with the plague. Also he was assessed on Danbury £800, and his estate sequestrated till payment was made, but eventually got off with payments of £163 and £100 after much litigation. The ship-money that he or his agents collected gave him trouble, as aforesaid, and no wonder, for he does not always pay over what he receives, thus :—

13 May, 1636. "Jo Olde brought with him £213, of which I paid £200 to His Majesty, the rest my wife had."

19 June, 1637. "Prynne deceased and would not crave a pardon."

Previously, on 10 May, he enters : "Prynne lost the other part of an ear in Cheapside." These are puzzling entries. One would suppose they referred to Wm. Prynne, the famous political pamphleteer, whose ears were twice cropped, but he did not die till 1669, so either the notice of death must be incorrect, or oddly enough there must have been two of the name whose ears were twice cut.

5 November, 1637. "The Morocquo Ambassador shall have his audience this day in all state,

I was with my Lady de la Warre there, durty,
a foolish sighte."

This was no doubt on the occasion when a letter
was brought for Charles I from Sidan, King of
Morocco, and the Ambassadors were entertained
with a masque and costly antic show through the
streets.

Sunday entertainments were still permitted.

26 November, 1637. "A cloudy day and sadd to
look upon. I am for the Church God speede
me there in his peace. After Evensonge at
the wrestlinge, good, very good."

This wrestling probably took place in the pleasant meadows outside the city walls.

April, 1638. "The Duchess of Chevreux came to
town and was Entertained with state by both
their Majesties."

November, 1638, he mentions seeing the Queen
Mother (Marie de' Medici) in town.

21 May, 1639, there were eclipses of the "sunn,"
which he goes to see on the Thames.

He often passed to and fro from Danbury to
London, and at the former place records :—

19 June, 1639. "Letter from Will Perry telling
of the fire at Queen Camel whereby 70 houses
were destroyed."

Perry was his Somersetshire agent.

16 August, 1639. "My brother (Sir Henry of
Wanstead) and his foolish lad came to dinner
and remained at this place, saw my bull and
dogges play."

He often mentions the baiting of his bull by dogs for his own amusement or that of his guests.

11 January, 1640. "To Maldon I am going to the Bayley's feaste, there I was and mett with base company and rascally saucy ministers."

16 February, 1640. "This morning His Ma: made the happy Act of triennial Parliaments."

11 March, 1640, he was again at Maldon with his brother Sir Henry, when the latter was elected Member of the Parliament which opened on the 13th April, and was dissolved on the 5th May.

June, 1640. "I dined at Marks my cozen Carewe Mildmayes and came to my wife in great heate, to Mr. Langhorne's where I mett her and came home, when I found their Majesties at supper with Madame Exceter and a many more."

So apparently his Royal Master was on very friendly terms with him.

August, 1640, he paid his first recorded visit to Queen Camel, riding by way of Oxford and Bath, then to London by the 22nd September, taking four days to ride by Swindon, Salisbury, Winchester, and Bagshot.

12 May, 1641. "Heard to the full of the good behaviour of the Earl of Strafforde, who died like a saint to the shame of his enemies."

6 June, 1641. "My wife to Graces among the puritans."

He mentions previously meeting "oulde Sir Henry Mildmay of Graces."

One of his many quarrels with his wife, but having an amicable ending, appears on

7 August, 1641. "Soon after dinner my woeman and I did fall out illfavouredly, and so we both continued sullen, till worthily I did acknowledge the error to be mine, when all became well againe, and we to supper and bedd."

He notes going to Bradley in Suffolk from Danbury with his wife and company, and adds :—" God be with me and us all, a longe journey."

He was always entertaining at dinner and supper, generally unexpected guests, and puts down on the

9 September, 1641 :—" to dinner came Sir Henry Mildmay and 40 with him, well feasted, danced and were merry till night."

This seems a large company to be called on to provide for suddenly, and very possibly one of the causes of disagreement with his wife was his constant hospitality.

The unpleasing entry appears on

17 February, 1642. "A rayleinge and lewd letter came to my wife from my brother Anthony by the footboye."

In May he again goes to Queen Camel and visits several places, including Bath, which he leaves

3 June, 1642. "Early up to be gonne, a heavy Parteinge, the wenches cried to lose their Danceinge, I spent my money freely."

He returned to Queen Camel, and war's alarms begin. The House of Commons ordered 27 August, 1642, the High Sheriff of Essex to go down and preserve the Lady Mildmay's house from plunderers at Danbery (*sic*), Sir Humphrey being absent.

3 September, 1642 :—" there hath been a battery all this day against the poor houses and town of Sherborne.   Master Hollis the man of mischief."

5 September, 1642. "The war is hot and blooddy, God amende it, to the leager where I was stopped and held 5 hours."

7 September, 1642. "To Sherborne I rode and saw the preparations of Sir Thomas Lamford and his men for Yeovil, towards night they fought it out stoutly, we have not heard what was done."

In after years, when King Charles II was proclaimed at Sherborne, 14 May, 1660, amid scenes of intense excitement, Sir John Strangways, as he rode through the streets, commended the people, and told them they were among the first in England to appear in arms for the defence of Charles I.

By the beginning of October, Sir Humphrey is back at Danbury.

25 October, 1642 :—" to Chelmsford in coach to see the foolery and impiety of the Earl of War(wick) and his rabble."

He was fifty on the 28th October.

3 November, 1642. "Home by newes of the devils
   abroad plundering."

4 November, 1642. "At home all day expecting
   the Barringtons and plunderers but I am safe
   as yet."

10 November, 1642. "Much company here at
   dinner, all in arms for the rogues."

His home life was not quite peaceful.

14 December, 1642 :—"timely up the air clear and
   most sweet, not far abroad but discontented,
   God helpe me, to dinner and not from home,
   all day wrangleing with her who has resolved
   long since not to amende, in peace to supper
   and bedd."

His drinking entries take this sort of form :—

13 February, 1643. ".Windy and cold, late in bedd,
   walking but not far, to dinner, soon after came
   Jo Griffith drunke, to tavern I wente with him
   and Parson Vincent, home to sup and bedd in
   peace."

He often plays cards at home, or as he sometimes calls them, "tables," and usually with the
parson.

14 April, 1643 :—"fair calm and growing, God helpe
   and deliver us from these troubles and trayters,
   late in bedd, to dinner, and then I wente forth
   towards night. I was forced to come away to
   hide."

2 May, 1643. "The Crosse in Cheape taken down
   by the Jews. The town in much disorder."

Sir Humphrey credits the Jews with the demoli-

tion of the Cross, but the contemporary account
says :—" The 2ᵈ May 1643 the Crosse in Cheapside
was pulled downe, a troope of horse and two com-
panies of foote wayted to garde it, and at the tope
crosse dromes beate, trumpets blew, and multitudes
of capes wayre throwne in the ayre ; and a great
shout of people with joy. The 2ᵈ of May the
Almanacke sayeth was the invention of the Crosse.
And to daye at night was the leaden popes burnt,
in the place where it stood, with ringing of bells,
and a great acclamation, and no hurt done in all
these actions."

So it was to the religious passions of the time
and not to the Jews that the destruction of the
Cross was due.

When in London in 1643 Sir Humphrey
generally dined at the "Trompett," no doubt a
hostelry, and such entries appear as :—" to dinner
at the Trompett with Sᵗ John and a many more,
and home well smitten with wine."

The troubled times caused many to leave.

12 August, 1643. "Wente to see my good friends
on board Shipp at Wapping in great misery."

Though a firm loyalist, his entries about the
rebellion are always short, and usually without
comment.

20 September, 1643. "His Majesty and R fought
at Newbury."

He was not of the Puritan form of religion, for
he has many invocations to the Blessed Virgin, and
writes :—

8 October, 1643. "Not to Church, the covenant being hot and I none of the tribe."

In April, 1644, he went to Queen Camel and was obliged to get a pass before starting. He rode by Maidenhead, Reading, Newbury, where he met the Army; then Marlborough, Chippenham, Bath, where, with one hundred others, he waited upon Her Majesty; thence to Bristol, and on the 23rd to Shappon and Camel, having started on the 16th.

17 June, 1644. "Good newes from Prince Rupert, Waller beaten well."

18 June, 1644. "At night came the rout and plundered my sword and bridles."

He allows himself to enter.

29 June, 1644 :—"by the help of God His Ma: shall flourish and his enemyes be confounded."

6 September, 1644:—"was a day of good newes concerning the Rebells, they are run from Ilchester to Dorsett, the Earl of Essex undone, and his Army scattered."

11 September, 1644. "Most unquiet, the villains came and had me, but I mad escape and fled to Wilton."

2 October, 1644:—"towards night came my Lo Cleveland with his brigade of horse to the 2 Camels to quarter."

His second son, whom he always calls Nompee, was appointed cornet of horse to his Lordship.

8 October, 1644. "I am to attend my Lords to the Rendezvous where I was and saw His Ma:, his train, Army, &c."

27 October, 1644. "This day poor Nompee was wounded."

This was at the second battle of Newbury.

11 February, 1645. He reports the capture of Weymouth by the Royal Forces.

30 March, 1645. "Col Nevill his regiment came and my house was abused by knaves."

8 July, 1645. "I rose and walked and soon after ran to Pilton with Nompee, where I lodged all night in feare."

10 July, 1645. "After dinner to Wrington in feare to a poor and lousy inn."

13 July, 1645:—"being Sunday I removed in feare towards the waterside at Bristol."

He then removes to Bath with his "crew," where he remains till the 31st, hearing bad news—fall of Bridgewater, etc.—goes to Possett in flight, next day with much "adoe," boated with horses to the Monmouthshire side, and the following day his son Nompee left to join the King at Cardiff. By the 3rd November he got safely back to London and goes "to the Club to sup," and several times refers to the Club, which, apparently, was held at the "Sun" tavern.

16 September, 1646. "All the talk of the death of the great Earle."

This refers to the Earl of Essex, who died suddenly of apoplexy on the 13th.

Humphrey now moved constantly to and from Danbury to London, but, evidently bored with his country life, was more and more addicted to being in London and, as he expresses it, "fuddling at a tavern," or, as he once writes, "to my ordinary trade of drinking."

12 November, 1646. He records the entry into London of Sir Thomas Fairfax.

15 December, 1646:—"remainder of the day preparing for Danbury by command of the House."

So apparently he was ordered home, whither he went by coach with Sir H. Chichley and Thomas Freemen, sleeping on the 17th at the "Cock" at Chelmsford.

11 March, 1647. A Mr. Arkenstall brought his pardon from the Lords and Commons, before whom he had several times attended when in London, and he was held in a bond for £184.

October, 1647. He notes the King's escape from London to the Isle of Wight.

22 December, 1647. He was present at the marriage of Henry Mildmay of Graces, but he was not fond of him, for he did not agree with his puritanical views, and in one place called him a rebel.

23 December, 1647. His son Charles died, but mourning for him did not last long, for he writes :—

6 January, 1648. "House full to dinner and no place but music and mirth all the day and night."

7 January, 1648. "As the day before less company, and after at night to Mother Podd's, the whole family, where we made debauch late."

Certainly it is strange to see such entries in a diary kept in a terrible period when every man's hand was against his neighbour.

September, 1648, he was in London with his man Snout and apparently made his peace with the Parliament.

17 October, 1648. "House of Commons my friends."

18 October, 1648. "My wife came with the joyful newes."

He is not grateful to her for he writes :—

19 October, 1648. "I lost my time with my wife at a play."

30 October, 1648. "Was at Goldsmith's Hall a fag end to all my troubles at that damned place."

He obtained on this occasion a draft order to clear him of this delinquency. In *Historical Sketches of Charles I, Cromwell, etc.*, there is a list of those who compounded for their estates, in which appears:—

"Sir Humphrey Mildemay of Danbury, Essex, £1275."

This was a heavy charge on him as his Danbury estate brought him in about £620 a year. When making a statement about his property he affirmed that he was never a popish recusant or popishly inclined. Loyalist as he is, the only note he makes of the beheading of his Royal Master is:—"Sadd newes of his Ma:"

13 April, 1652. "I putt on mourning for oulde Mary."

This was Lady Crofts, his wife's mother, who died on the 18 February.

23 April, 1652. "I rode to Chelmsford to my brother Sir Henry the great man."

Sir Henry, who had gone over to the Revolutionary party, was probably instrumental in making his brother's peace with Parliament.

This first part of the diary ends on the 9th July, 1652, when Sir Humphrey was in London. There are references in it to various relations. His brother, Sir Henry, who lived at Whitehall and Wanstead ; brother Anthony, who lived at Whitehall ; cousin Charles (great uncle to the first Lord FitzWalter), who lived at Chelsea ; Ambrose, son of Walter Mildmay of Much Baddow ; cozen Robert Mildmay of Moulsham ; old Father Robert Mildmay of Terling ; Sir Walter Mildmay ; Sir John and Lady Mildmay ; Lady Crofts, his wife's mother, who had a house at (Bednal) Bethnal Green ; his cousins Argal ; Bennett ; Jo: Stocker : Will Capell ; Greenfield ; and Appleton. He also mentions the deaths of old Sir Henry Mildmay of Graces, 9 October, 1639 ; and Lady Mildmay of Moulsham, 8 February, 1640.

In the *Life of General Richard Deane*, by John Bathurst Deane, 1870, there is a Deane pedigree showing that Jane, daughter of Sir Richard Deane,

Lord Mayor, married Robert Mildmay of Terling, Essex, and the author says :—"The three daughters of Sir Richard Deane married into three of the most Republican families of the time, Rolfe, Mildmay, and Goodwin."

Some items of prices may be gathered from the diary :— 2 coach horses cost £18 ready cash ; a horse at pasture cost 3/- a week ; piece of velvet 37 y<sup>ds</sup> long 19<sup>d</sup> a yard ; 2 dozen small candles 12/- (beinge very dear) ; 3 quarts of the best sallet oyle 7/- ; and he sold his " velvett " bed to Thomas Chickley for £80. To M<sup>r</sup> Gunter he paid 1/4 for peas and strawberries ; a leg of mutton cost 10<sup>d</sup> ; and tobacco 1/- an ounce. The theatre cost 1/- and 1/6. It would be interesting to know whether the Mr. Gunter referred to was an ancestor of the well-known Gunter of Berkeley Square.

In the diary are certain expressions not easy of interpretation, and the kindness of the Editor permitted their insertion in *Notes and Queries* with a request for help towards explaining them.

They are as follows :—

" To Church againe, and after supper to the *Spaniards discipline*, and to bedd."

" Morrisen putt on me a new suit of *parragen*."

" Measured the pale."

" Captain Marcie came to me and was despatched by the *defaulte of his compliment*."

" To Putleigh I rode and remained there all day to *putt* for the poore children."

" Danceing the ropes."

"Sir Will Waler the Conqueror to London" July
   1643.

"To my Camel where I *beate sticke* and came home."

In *Notes and Queries*, 10 S. II., page 533, were
   these answers :—

"Parragen."   By this I presume parragone is intended, which is a richly embroidered cloth
   imported principally from Turkèy.

"Dancing the ropes." To be hanged.

"To putt for the poore children." Putt, a silly fellow,
   a clown, an oddity.

   (Signed)   EVERARD HOME COLEMAN.

Perhaps the "Spaniards Discipline" was of the
religious observances partially introduced by Philip
of Spain.

A "parragen" is probably a burracan, a kind of
   woollen stuff, a sort of camlet of which coat
   and trousers were made.

"Measured the pale." Looked to his expenditure.
   To leap the pale was to exceed in one's
   expenses.   Halliwell.

A "compliment" was a gift or present.  Captain
Marcie seems to have been shown the door in default of something of the kind.

Possibly when Sir Humphrey rode to Putleigh,
and remained there all day to "putt" for the poor
children, he went to amuse them by means of a
game of cards, now obsolete, called putt.

"Dancing the ropes."   Would not this be an item
   of expenditure devoted to the pleasures of the

time.   Pepys recalls going to see Jacob Hall's dancing on the ropes.

"To beat sticke."   Query to depart, like to beat the hoof, i.e. to depart.

(Signed)    F. HOLDEN MacMICHAEL.

"A new suit of parragen," i.e. parragon, q.v. N.E.D.

"Sir Will Waler."   Sir William Waller, q.v. D.N.B.

(Signed)    W. C. B.

We cannot feel altogether satisfied with these explanations.   "Parragen" may very possibly be barragon, which with serges and other woven fabrics was manufactured at Alton, Hants.

"Dancing the ropes" may refer to some performer dancing on ropes, but not to the execution of criminals, for Sir Humphrey, in his diary, mentions several times the hanging of offenders, and always says they were hanged.   He would not be likely on a single occasion to use a vulgar and rather brutal expression.

In our opinion "putting" for the poor children meant some form of voting for them when they were being drawn or selected as apprentices.

We have never heard the expression "to beat the hoof," but are familiar with "to pad the hoof."

As for Sir William Waller, we believe he was in Ireland in July, 1643, nor does the D.N.B. contradict this.

The second part of Sir Humphrey's diary running from 11 July, 1652, to 2 June, 1666, is among the Marquis of Ormonde's papers at Kilkenny Castle. Mr. C. Litton Falkiner was kind enough to examine this thoroughly, and reported that the diary contains nothing of interest, being merely a chronicle of the weather and of the diarist's health. From the extracts Mr. Falkiner was so good as to send, this can be clearly seen ; also that by 1665 the writer was an invalid, for the entries of " In bed and by the fyre " run consecutively day after day. When the diary closes Sir Humphrey was nearly seventy-four years of age, and probably did not live much longer.

Sir Humphrey's eldest son John was both a soldier and a Commissioner of Excise for the county of Essex. A helmet bearing the Mildmay lion, which hangs in Danbury Church, is supposed to have been his. In his military capacity he was with the Royal troops in Colchester when that town was besieged, was taken prisoner on the surrender, and it is amusing to imagine that he may have been given into the custody of his cousin Carew Hervey Mildmay of Marks, who commanded a Parliamentary regiment on this occasion.

He was imprisoned for a time, but freed upon his parole to appear any time within six months, after six days' warning, to be left at his father's house of Danbury. His horses were delivered to him on payment of their charges.

A reminder of this same siege came to light in 1905, for while an ancient shop was undergoing

H

repairs, massive oaken beams were found thickly studded with bullets fired during the siege.

As Excise Commissioner John had much trouble with his office which he farmed. He was discharged from it by Parliament in 1665, and apparently there were claims against him on account of it, for after the Restoration we find in the Treasury accounts, 5 December, 1661 :— "Allowance to Colonel John Mildmay Commissioner of Excise for Essex of £100 for losses." In February, 1662–3 he got £400 more, and 31 January, 1664 :—"Warrant from Treasurer Southampton to the Excise Commissioners to discharge John Mildmay of his debt of £68–10–0 as a Farmer of some part of the Excise, for which said Mildmay is in prison, and his security Thomas Killigrew is being sued in the Exchequer. All in consideration of Mildmay's sufferings and faithful services." Even then he does not go free, for on 6 May, 1665, there is another warrant from Treasurer Southampton to the Excise Commissioners to discharge John Mildmay, a Sub-Commissioner, of an arrear of £136 19s. 6d., he having been long a prisoner in the King's Bench, all in consideration of his services to the late King in the late war. Let us hope that this last order procured his release.

John married, in 1665, Mary Bancroft, inherited the Danbury property, had no children, left Danbury to his widow, who took as her second husband Dr. Croly, by whom she had one daughter, who married Wm. Fytche, when Danbury passed to that family, and subsequently to many other owners.

The modern house was built by Mr. Round, who, in 1832, pulled down the one built by Sir Walter Mildmay, known in his time as Deenbury Place. Nothing now remains of the Mildmay period, except perhaps some of the trees, for there are grand old oaks standing in Danbury Park, possibly dating back to Sir Humphrey's time.

In 1845 Danbury was purchased by the Ecclesiastical Commissioners, and was for some time an Episcopal residence.

The Fytche family possessed a portrait of Humphrey Mildmay of Danbury, æt. 7 anno. 1599, of which there is an Indian ink drawing in the Dogmersfield scrap-book.

John's tombstone in Danbury Church records :— "Hic jacet | Joannes Mildmay Armiger | filius Humfredi Mildmay | Milites in comitatu Essexiæ | obitt 10 August 1673."

Sir Humphrey's second and favourite son, so often referred to in the diary as Nompee, evidently a pet version of Humphrey, was made heir to the Queen Camel estate.

Camel was a common river-name among the Britons, and Queen added from the manor, having belonged to the Queen of William the Conqueror.

In 1660 there was a grant for peppercorn rent of Hazlegrove farm to Wm. Parker, of London, for ninety-nine years, in consideration of the marriage of Humphrey Mildmay and Sarah, sister of Wm. Parker. This was Nompee's second wife.

She is buried in Westminster Abbey under a wrong name. In the register of burials in the Abbey appears :—" 1700-1 Jan. 17 M⁣ʳˢ Dorothy Mildmay, widow, in the South Cross, at the entrance to Sᵗ Benedict's Chapel."

In Colonel Chester's register of Marriages, Baptisms, and Burials in St. Peter's Church, Westminster, there is this note :—

" The Christian name in the register is wrong, and should be Sarah. In an original affidavit of her burial in woollen, curiously preserved among the Abbey muniments, dated 22 Jan 1700/1, she is called 'M⁣ʳˢ Sarah Mildmay of the parish of Crist Church in the City of London.' In her will dated 2 Jan 1700/1 she was described as ' Sarah Mildmay, widow, relict of Humphrey Mildmay of Queen Camel, Co Somerset, Esqre,' and she directed to be buried in the Abbey Church of Sᵗ Peter in Westminster, while an affidavit in her handwriting states that the will was written on that day ' at her lodging in the house of M⁣ʳ Dewe in Warwick lane,' which is in the parish of Christchurch. There can be therefore no doubt as to her identity, so that there was an inadvertent error in the Abbey register. She left £100 for her funeral expenses, and £10 to the poor of the parish of Plympton, Co Devon, where she was born. The will was proved 14 March 1700/1 by her Executor Francis

Nixon. She was the youngest daughter of Edmund Parker, Co Devon, was unmarried at the date of her father's will in 1642, and was probably upwards of seventy years of age at her death."

In the church at Hazlegrove is a tablet bearing the Mildmay arms and inscribed :—

"Near this place lyeth the body of Humphrey Mildmay Esqre, Lord of this manor, second son of Sir Humphrey Mildmay of Danbury in the County of Essex. He sustained several wounds in the wars for his loyalty to his Prince King Charles I, particularly at Newbury fight, where he served as Major under his uncle the Earl of Cleveland, and was taken up among the slain. His first wife was Sarah the daughter of Thomas Freke Esqre of Honiton, St Mary, Dorsetshire. His second wife was Sarah daughter of Edmund Parker of Borringdon in Devonshire. He died on the 19th November 1690, aged 67, and having no issue, left his estate to his kinsman Carew Hervey Mildmay of Marks, who in token of his gratitude erected this monument."

# ANTHONY MILDMAY

ONE of the boon companions of Sir Humphrey the diarist, was his brother Anthony, of whose early life nothing much is known, but he very probably was the Anthony Mildmay who was Member for Westlow, Cornwall, in 1640.

He was attached to the Court, being one of the sewers or table attendants to King Charles I; Wood calls him carver, and he was very constant in his attendance on that monarch when in confinement.

The following letter of Anthony Mildmay to his brother, Sir Henry, is interesting as showing his own opinion of the services he had rendered and their inadequate reward, and his opinion of his King, with that King's opinion of Sir Henry. It is taken from the *Clarke Papers*, Camden Society publications, and was first printed 27 April–8 May, 1648, in the *Mercurius Veridicus*, a Royalist paper.

" My worthy good Brother

" I am resolved to continue here one month more to see what time will produce, but longer I

CAPTAIN ANTHONY MILDMAY

will not stay upon the terms I am now, my danger being very great and certain, and my reward uncertain; for you may well conceive that the malignant party will be still practising against me, to make me suspected of the Parliament and their Army, hoping to remove me by that means : all other ways they practised in vain. Many things are omitted in the last declaration which I hope you will mention in the next. Some little time before the first expedition against the Scots, Ship-money and other taxes coming in slow, it was resolved by the King (at a juncto) that a regiment of horse should be presently raised, the pretence for a Guard for the King's person ; but there was no need of that, there being a band of Pensioners and the Yeomen of the Guard. The old Countesse of Devonshire paid £2,000 to Marquess Hamilton, which he was to have as a gift when this Lord Wilmot was established Commander in Chief of that regiment. If Mʳ Haughton an Attorney living in St. James and one Mʳ Barrow that lives in Cheneys in Buckinghamshire, Sir Edward Worthey and Faye Wortley be examined they will satisfie the Parliament that this horseguard was to be imployed absolutely to force the King's will upon the people. Sir, this day, our worthy Governor and the King had some disputes in my hearing and others. In short, the King had very many bitter expressions against your proceedings, and said, that any King that should do such abominable things as you did deserved to have his Crown pulled off his head. I was astonished to hear him say so ; for formerly his opinion was that no king could deserve to be deposed ; that he was accomptable to none but God : Who then should pull off his Crown ? He said that the passing of the Act to make Strafford a traitor lay heavie on his conscience. That it was the greatest sin he ever committed, that he was forced to do it, and if he had the power, he would say the same against all the Acts he had passed this Parliament. In some of his Declarations from Oxford he expresseth with what freedome hee passed all the Acts that hee passed this Parliament, and if they were to passe, hee would passe them, and now you hear hee professed the contrary in the hearing of divers of us. He is the most perfidious man that ever lived, and if he ever gets power, he will make no more difficulty to hang you than I will to eat my dinner this cold day. Our charge is great and dangerous, our attendance insupportable, did not God enable us. You know what discouragements I have when strangers are placed before me, and although they be honest men, yet they have not performed the service to Parliament that I have. I was servant to King James in an honorable condition, and to this King ever since he was crown'd, and yourself and all who know me must affirm that I was ever a great opponent of tyranny and Popery. Eighteen years since I was sworn Gent of the Privie Chamber, and so continued, and now I am lesse, and must so continue or come away.

I desire your advice without which I will do nothing.

> "Your brother and Servant
>
> "A. MILDMAY

"Carrisbrook, 29 Feb: 1647."

On the 21st March, 1648, Anthony writes from Windsor Castle to Mr. Faulconbridge, His Majesty's Receiver-General, asking £100 in payment of official services, and John Creyke receipts the same paper as receiving the £100 for Captain Mildmay, in respect to the said Captain's allowance of £200 per annum as one of the four gentlemen attending the King in the Isle of Wight.

There was a warrant from Parliament on the 9th July, 1648, to bring up in safe custody Captain Anthony Mildmay, but he soon made his peace, probably through the influence of his brother, Sir Henry, and on the 30th November, 1648, Lieut.-Colonel Cobbett came with Anthony Mildmay to the door of the King's chamber at Newport, and made a great knocking. On the Duke of Richmond, who was in attendance, enquiring what it meant, Mildmay made answer that some of the officers of the army wished to see the King. They were admitted, the King arrested and taken from the Isle of Wight.

The trial and condemnation of the King soon followed, and a week after the execution the body of the King, embalmed and coffined in lead, was confided to Anthony Mildmay, Mr. Herbert,

another of the sewers, Captain Preston, and John
Joynen, formerly cook to Charles I, and by them
taken in a hearse to Windsor, and placed in that
which formerly was the King's bedchamber. (See
Heath's *Chronicles*.)   In the statement rendered
of expenses incurred the hearse is called a chariot.
Mr. Herbert resolved to bury Charles I in the
vault under the monument to King Edward IV,
and gave orders for the opening thereof, but the
Duke of Richmond, Marquess of Hertford, Earl
of Southampton, and Earl of Lindsey coming to
Windsor to perform their last duty to the King's
memory, had the body placed in a hollow where
were the coffins of King Henry VIII and Queen
Jane, his third wife.   Bishop Juxon was present
to perform the office of burial, but Colonel
Whitchot, the Governor of the Castle, would not
suffer it.

No mention is made of Anthony Mildmay at
the burial.   He probably was not of sufficient
social importance to join such great nobles, besides
being regarded as a very doubtful Royalist.

He received £10 for mourning cloth on the
occasion.

Anthony signed the true inventory of all the
horses belonging to Titbury Race, being part of
the late King's personal estate, taken 24 July, 1649.
There were 102 horses, valued at £1982. (See
*Newmarket*, by Hore.)

He was active in dealing with the valuables in
the Jewel Houses, as appears from the release to his

brother, Sir Henry, quoted in the account of that brother, and from a paper dated 25 September, 1649 :—

"Ye trustees names who took away the King's plate out of the Jewel House both at Whitehall and the Tower.

GEO: WITHERS ⎱ The Keys of the Tower to
ANT: MILDMAY ⎰ be delivered to them.
And seven others."

By the advice of Sir Henry the younger children of the late King were committed .to Captain Anthony's custody. In July, 1650, instructions were given to him by the Council of State to remove the late King's children from the care of the Countess of Leicester at Pencester (Penshurst) to Carisbrook Castle, in the Isle of Wight, and he was ordered to go with his wife and take the Duke of Gloucester and his sister and receive £200 on account for his expenses. This he did, and in September the Princess Elizabeth died, as reported in the *Modern Intelligencer*, September 10–18, 1650.

"Thursday, September 12. This day came certain news from the Isle of Wight of the death of Lady Elizabeth Stuart daughter of the late King, who being at bowls, a sport she much delighted in, there fell a sudden shower which caused her to take cold, being of a sickly constitution, she fell into a feverish distemper, which notwithstanding the care and industry of that faithful gentleman Mr. Anthony Mildmay, and all the arts of physicians, being naturally of a weak body, and

her fever growing strong upon her, She departed
this life on Sunday 8 September."

She probably had not much chance of recovery,
for Captain Anthony wrote to the Council that
Carisbrook was bleak and cold, and may be pre-
judicial to health, and as, according to Hume, the
Commons intended to apprentice the Princess to a
button-maker, it was perhaps as well that she died.

The leaden coffin containing the remains of the
Princess was found in 1793, when digging a grave
in the chancel of Newport Church for the inter-
ment of a brother of Lord Delawar.

She died in her sixteenth year, and is said to
have been found dead with her face resting on an
open Bible, a Bible she much loved, for it was
given to her by her father.    She is thus represented
on the marble monument erected to her memory
by Her Majesty Queen Victoria.

In the same month of September the Duke of
Gloucester, or, as he is now called, Henry Stuart,
is to go to Heidelberg, and Captain Anthony is
desired to send one of the Duke's servants to
receive money for the journey, but there seems
reason to believe that Mildmay opposed the Duke's
departure, not caring probably to be deprived of
the money he received for acting as custodian.  But
he was kind to the Duke, and on good terms with
him, as appears from the following letter :—

"S' I hope you remember the promise you made
to me when you went from hence.  My liberty

will not be granted yet methinkes, some enlarge-
ment should, and I not be thought to intend my
pleasure more than my health in desiring it. You
can best judge how far it will be best to proceede
in my behalfe, I would have nothing askt that may
be thought unfitt nor anything that is not so if
likely to displease. This you may be sure of and
therefore not doubt to use your own liberty (without regard to myne) in considering first what is
safe, then the satisfaction and benefit of your

" loveing friend

" H. GLOUCESTER."

Some time after this, that is, in February, 1653,
Colonel Sydenham, Governor of the Isle of Wight,
informed Cromwell that Mr. Lovell had procured
a vessel to convey Henry Stuart to Flanders, but
complains that Mildmay, without a particular order
from Parliament, refuses " to let the child out of
his custody, and keeps him close locked up within
the compass of his own lodgings."

Mr. Percy G. Stone in *Architectural Antiquities
of the Isle of Wight* goes on to state "that the
determination was against the young Duke's wishes
is apparent from a letter addressed by him to the
Council of State, which concluded with a request
that Colonel Sydenham may be allowed to hasten
his departure despite opposition on Mildmay's part.
This letter had the desired effect, and in February,
1653, the Duke sailed from Cowes for Flanders."

Frequent petitions for arrears of money were sent

by Anthony Mildmay. On the 25th November, 1650, he rendered account of money received for the care and keep of Prince Henry and Princess Elizabeth, children of the late King, from 9 August to 22 November at £3000 a year. On the death of the Princess the cost of keep was lessened by the discharge of four servants only. He had expended in extras £100 for the journey from Penshurst to the Isle of Wight; £100 in repairing and furnishing Carisbrook Castle; £80 for medical attendance and personal charges for the late Princess, and for a leaden coffin, vault, and journey to London to acquaint the Council with her sickness; £32 2s. 6d. for gentlemen attending the Council. Total, £312 2s. 6d., which is ordered to be paid to him.

After the death of the Princess the allowance for the care of Henry Stuart was reduced to £1500, and Captain Anthony sent the following letter on behalf of the Princess' servants :—

" May it please your Honour

" In obedience to the Council of State I took care of the late King's children, one of which, the Lady Elizabeth, being since deceased, and her four servants allowed by the Council being thereupon discharged, they are now Petitioners to the Parliament to be taken into consideration, according to their own noble presidents (sic) in like cases.

" These things having fallen out during my

unhappy employment, and having found the
Petitioners deportment to be very civil and
inoffensive, and humbly conceiving them fit objects
of the Parliament's compassion, do presume to
make it my very humble suit, that your Honours
will please to vouchsafe them what charitable
Favour their necessitous Behaviour (rectius
condition) seemed to begge.

"And I am the rather encouraged to become
thus troublesome from the Assurance I have of
your Honour's goodness ; acknowledging with
great thankfulness the many Favours you have
been pleased formerly to honour me with. To all
which if you shall please to make the Addition,
and pardon this too great Boldness, Obligation of
Gratitude and Duty will be much increased upon
Your Honours most faithful servant.

" A. MILDEMAY, Carisbrook Castle, Oct. 28, 1650.

(1) John Barniston, her Gentleman Usher
(2) Judith Briott, her Gentlewoman
(3) Elizabeth Janes, her Laundrie Mayde
(4) John Clarke, Groom of the Chamber

"To the Honourable W^m Lenthall Esqre Speaker
in Parliament."

In August, 1654, he sent another petition asking
that his arrears of £269 19s. may be paid to him,
which arrears he did not get.

After the Restoration there was an indictment
and conviction of Anthony Mildmay on the
24th July, 1661, for embezzling plate and goods

belonging to the late King, and in October, 1661, Colonel Sydenham was relieved of his office, and the persons of Anthony Mildmay and others attached.

On the 17th September, 1662, there was a grant to Hastwait Wright and eleven other officers and sufferers in the late King's service, of a third part of certain concealed goods, jewels, money, etc., discovered by them, viz. plate, hangings, etc., delivered to Anthony Mildmay of Newington Green, Middlesex, for the use of the Duke of Gloucester and Princess Elizabeth, at Carisbrook Castle, but converted to his own use.

Lastly, 15 May, 1663, warrant to Anthony Mildmay, who is indebted to the King £1950 for plate taken at Carisbrook Castle belonging to the Crown, and has paid one-third to Richard Pight, the discoverer, to pay the other two-thirds to Charles Wheeler and others and compound with them for the same.

The epithet, "a knave at heart," which Mr. Stone in his book applies to Anthony Mildmay, seems hardly deserved, for, no doubt, he only followed the general example in appropriating part of the late King's possessions, and, in his case, this was possibly done to make good arrears of money due to him for the expenses of his custody of the late King's children.

By an order of Council plate was given out for the use of the young Prince and Princess when they were under the charge of Anthony Mildmay, and this doubtless is the plate he was accused of embezzling.

According to a paper presented to the House of Lords in 1660, he also took possession of the so-called Unicorn's horn that was at Windsor.

Anthony's signature is to be seen on a paper at Dogmersfield, being a release to his brother, Sir Henry, and the writing is very good.

There was a picture of Captain Anthony Mildmay at Moulsham. This has disappeared, but a very good small Indian ink drawing of it is in the Dogmersfield scrap-book.

He apparently acquired the title of Captain before the Civil War, and during that war commanded No. 34 troop of horse, under the Parliamentary Commander the Earl of Bedford.

His wife's Christian name was Anne, and she is mentioned in the will of her sister-in-law, wife of Sir Henry Mildmay.

She was possibly the Anne Murrey, who married an Anthony Mildmay 27 February, 1648-9, but we have not discovered whether she had any children, nor where or when Captain Anthony died.

I

# SIR HENRY MILDMAY OF
# WANSTEAD

THE most notorious of the brothers of
Sir Humphrey the diarist was Henry,
who, though a very young man, was
appointed Master of the Jewel Office in
1609, and held that position under James I and
Charles I, having a residence in Whitehall. In a
private letter of the time he is said to have bought
the appointment for £2000 or £3000. This is
very possible, for though the fees actually due to
the Master of the Jewel Office only amounted to
£50 yearly, Henry Mildmay, from the fees he
himself instituted, received at the rate of £250 a
year during his term of office, altogether about
£10,000.

He belonged to Gray's Inn, was one of the
King's sewers, and was knighted 9 August, 1617.

Judging by the entries in the Domestic State
Papers, one of Sir Henry's principal duties was to
find money by pawning or selling plate and jewels,
and it is very probable that he caused to be sold
one of the most remarkable of the jewels that were
in the Tower in the reign of James I. This was a
gold jewel set with a very large diamond, a ruby
to match, and two other diamonds, one being

known as the "Stone of Scotland," and the jewel was called the "Mirror of Great Britain."

There must have been a large quantity of plate in the Jewel House not required by the Royal Households, for not only was Sir Henry allowed the use of some at Whitehall and Wanstead, but others had the same privilege, and it was freely given away.

A paper signed by Sir Henry gives some idea of the expenditure on plate, for it authorises the payment of £6786 to John Acton, Goldsmith to the King, for gilt plate, chains, and medals of gold to Ambassadors, and for repairs of plate, for the year ending 25 March, 1637. This is a large sum considering the difference in the value of money at that date and now.

Sir Henry was brought up at Court, excelled in manly exercises, and Clarendon terms him :—"A great flatterer of all persons in authority."

He was a man about town, much in society, and not over strict in his behaviour, as may be learnt from a picture of him on a pack of political playing-cards, of which there is a facsimile in the Guildhall.

In the will of the eccentric Philip, Earl of Pembroke, there is this clause:—" then seeing that I did menace a certain Henry Mildmay but did not thrash him, I do leave the sum of £50 sterling to the lacquey that shall pay my debt."

Sir Henry married 6 April, 1619, Anne, daughter and coheir of William Haliday, mercer and Alderman of London, and this marriage was mainly brought about by the following letter from King James I to Alderman Haliday :—

"JAMES REX

"Trusty and well beloved we greet you well. We understand that Sir Henry Mildmay our servant, is a suitor to your daughter, who, for his person and other external parts may well appear to you worthy of the match with any gentlewoman of good quality. As for our opinion of him it may be seen by this, that we have preferred him from a place of ordinary attendance about our person, to a place of great charge and trust, which we never before bestowed on a man of his years ; and therefore we can not but wish him all advancement of his fortunes, and particularly in that match with your daughter, whereunto, if ye shall give it your best furtherance, you shall not only give us good cause of acknowledging your respect unto us herein, but as we have been and will be a father unto him, so will we unto your daughter.

"Given at our Court at Theobalds, fourth day, Oct: 1618.

"If ye knew how far your conformity to our pleasure in this will be acceptable unto us, and profitable to yourselves, you would be willinger to perform it than we to desire it of you, for ye may be sure that however this may succeed, we will prefer him to a better place than he yet hath."

Probably Sir Henry found the Mastership of

PANELLED ROOM, TEMP: JAMES I, MILDMAY HOUSE, ISLINGTON

the Jewel Office too profitable a post to relinquish it for any other, for he certainly got no preferment from King James I ; but the "better place" referred to by that King may have been made up to him in other ways, for, according to *Court and Times of James I* :—" Monday last week Sir Henry Mildmay married Alderman Haliday's daughter, and has received in free gift from His Majesty, as they say, two manors worth £12,000 to make his estate somewhat proportionate to his wife's."

Sir Henry settled on his wife the manor of Wanstead, Essex, then valued at £1000 a year, which he bought with her money in 1619 from George, Duke of Buckingham, and where he afterwards entertained James I. When writing from there Sir Henry calls the place " Wonstead."

According to Lysons old Wanstead house is introduced in the background of a picture of Queen Elizabeth at Welbeck. A very small print of this house was published by Stent in 1649.

Alderman Wm. Haliday had a house, pasture ground, and park of forty-four acres at Newington Green. The westernmost part of the house still stands, and in it are three rooms handsomely wainscoted in oak. In one is a carved mantelpiece, having in the centre a shield bearing 3 esquires' helmets, 2 and 1, the arms of Haliday, and its ceiling wrought in stucco contains the arms of England and I.R. (James I), medallions of Hector, Alexander, etc. The other two wainscoted rooms have also carved mantelpieces, but, alas, the whole of the woodwork is thickly covered with paint.

This house and the surrounding property came to Sir Henry's wife after the Alderman's death, and was a country residence. Even in 1754 the place was well separated from town, for a newspaper advertisement of that date, after recommending a house at Newington Green for refreshments, ends with:—"A sixpenny coach to and from London every day."

This property, which passed from Mildmay possession in 1857, acquired the family name, being still known as Mildmay Park. The house has had many vicissitudes, at one time being the Mildmay boarding school, and it is now occupied by the Mildmay Deaconesses belonging to a religious and charitable institution.

A general pardon to Sir Henry Mildmay is among the Dogmersfield papers, dated 1 Car: i, Feb: 10.

This monarch presented to him four full-length pictures, now at Dogmersfield—King James I ; Sir Thomas Vere, Lord Tilbury ; Villiers, Duke of Buckingham ; and Gustavus Adolphus. In a memorandum dated 1774, by Carew Hervey Mildmay of Hazlegrove, he states that those pictures, then at Hazlegrove, were by different painters, King James being by Rubens, Lord Tilbury and the Duke of Buckingham by Van Dyck, the artist of the picture of Gustavus Adolphus being unknown. He adds that this last picture was brought to King Charles I by the Marquis of Hamilton, who received it from Gustavus himself as a present to the King. Mr. Carew Mildmay further states that it is supposed to be the only portrait existing of Gustavus Adolphus, but there is a small picture of that great man by Van Dyck in the gallery at Munich.

An examination of the three pictures first named shows that they are not by the master hands of Rubens and Van Dyck, and it is more probable that they were painted by Cornelius Janssen, to whom they are generally attributed.

Another picture at Dogmersfield of the same heroic size is a fine full-length portrait of Prince Rupert by Sir Peter Lely, and this was probably acquired at the same time.

When Emmanuel College was threatened Sir Henry came forward to protect its privileges, for there is a letter from Charles I to the Vice-Chancellor and Heads of the University of Cambridge, dated 5 May, 1627, to the following effect :—
The King by his Royal prerogative suspends a statute of Emmanuel College for the removal of fellows. Sir Henry Mildmay, grandson of the founder, being desirous to maintain the suspended statute, had offered to annex five or six new benefices to the College, and it is provided that if he do so within six years the present suspension shall be revoked.

Various opportunities like the following were given to Mildmay for acquiring money :—

4 August, 1630, Charles I to Sir Henry Mildmay and Sir T. Fanshawe, commission for com-
pounding with persons appointed to receive knighthood.   They to be collectors.

Sir Henry wrote from Twyford 9 October, 1638,
to Sir J. Coke, Principal Secretary of State :—

" I had not absented myself so long from Court
had not the hand of God hindered ; and it hath
pleased God to restore me into a reasonable way of
recovery.   My wife who was the cause under God
of cherishing me in my sickness is fallen desper-
ately ill herself which causes me to make some
stay from my attendance upon His Majesty to give
that reciprocal comfort that becomes an honest husband to so good a wife in this country where I am
loath to leave her as a stranger.   This truth I
humbly desire you to present to His Majesty
which is the best present a faithful servant can give
to his Master."

It seems curious that he should refer to Twyford, which belonged to his wife, as a place where
she was a stranger.

Sir Henry was Member for Maldon, and ever
ready to come forward in Parliament.   He took
part in the great debate of the 6 August, 1625, on
the foreign policy of the Crown, and as a friend
of Buckingham, whose honesty and policy were
attacked, proposed a vote for a sum of money for
the equipment of the fleet against Spain.

In the course of George Villiers, Duke of
Buckingham's, answer to his impeachment on the

8th June, 1626, he says :—" With reference especially to the Earl of Middlesex who was said to have paid him six thousand pounds for the Mastership of the Wards, he could prove that this sum had afterwards been given by the Earl to his late Majesty who bestowed it on Sir Henry Mildmay without the Duke's priority, and he had it and enjoyed it."

In Sir Henry's time members who were not in their places by 8 a.m., the hour for prayers, were fined 1s., and on the 8th May, 1641, the Speaker did not arrive till 9.30. Sir Henry at once stood up and said he did hope the Speaker hereafter would come in time, whereupon the Speaker threw twelve pence upon the table and declined to take them up again.

In the same year of 1641 Sir Henry voted against the attainder of the Earl of Strafford.

In the Parliament of 1642 he subscribed £600 towards the loan for the relief of Ireland, that is, for the suppression of the rebellion there, to which fund Oliver Cromwell subscribed £500.

In 1647–8 he made a long speech in favour of Argyll, and moved that he be paid his £10,000, and the rest of the Scottish debts be continued at 8 per cent.

When accompanying the King with the army on the borders of Scotland, Sir Henry's letters to Secretary Windebank are laudatory of His Majesty. Thus, 24 May, 1639, he writes :—" Our blessed Master is in perfect health, and the most active and vigilant Prince in his affairs that I think lives"; and 10 June :—"The King carries himself with as great wisdom and courage as is possible, it is a thousand pities he should want anything"; but he evidently does not wish to be bound by what he writes, for the letter ends :—"I beseech you burn this letter."

The receipt of favours and strongly expressed admiration of the King could not induce Sir Henry Mildmay to adhere to the Royal cause, and his letters show how early he sided with the Parliament against his "Blessed Master."

On the 18th October, 1643, he wrote to Sir William Mason and the other Deputy Lieuts. of Essex :—

"hast, post hast, let the two bearers pass. We have received two letters from you both of one date. The alarum of the enemies approach towards our associated Counties was very hot with us before yours came. My Lord General and the Council of War took your advertisements very kindly, especially your last, which mentions the assistance of your foot. They have resolved to send 36 troops of horse, and 50 dragoniers and desire you to give what assistance you can of men according to your offer, but speed must be the life of this action. I know you will consider it. The troops go away within these 6 hours. Be careful of your Officers. My Lord General looks for his £300 which he laid out of his purse, and takes it ill he is not paid. My Lord Fairfax hath seconded my

Lord Manchester's overthrow with another, and he hath beaten the enemy out of Hull.

"P.S. The Parliament expects that you should levy all arrears due in the County rigorously and with expedition, and the estates of papists not be neglected. I hope my brother Humphrey will not be liable to have his estate sequestered for his son's delinquency."

Sir Humphrey's son was serving with the army of the King.

In the Dogmersfield library there was a manuscript official copy of the Minute Book of the secret meetings of the Revolutionary Junto or Parliamentary Committee, sitting chiefly at the "White Harte" in Romford. This copy was made for Sir Henry Mildmay, who was one of the Secret Committee.

Sir Henry appealed to anyone in authority whichever side he was on, for in May, 1644, he wrote to Walter Ashton, Ambassador for the King in Spain, praying him to use his influence to free George Daker seized by the Inquisition.

Sir Henry being a man of great wealth was ordered to be present at York on the 15th of January, 1647, to be delivered to the Scottish Army as one of the hostages for the payment of £200,000 for which they sold the King. He to be detained as hostage seven days at the utmost.

So far did Sir Henry's partizanship carry him that he was one of the judges of King Charles I, and in consequence is always referred to in the family as the Regicide.

He sat on the trial on the 6th, 10th, 15th, 20th, 23rd (twice), 25th, and 26th January, 1648–9, eight times out of the twenty-two sittings—once in Westminster Hall, the other times in the Painted Chamber, and Nalson says made violent speeches against the King.

He did not sign the death warrant, nor was he present on the 27th when sentence of death was passed.

He was appointed with two others to make all arrangements for providing provisions and necessaries for the King and the President of the Court, and the Sword of State being in his custody, he was ordered to deliver it to John Humphrey, Esq., to be borne before the Lord President.

Sir Henry may have been one of those who were dissatisfied with the resolution arrived at not to hear the King in the Painted Chamber before sentence, and therefore withdrawn from the trial, as did Colonel Harvey and some others of the Commissioners.

The Commonwealth Government considered him a man of importance ; so, although fully aware that he was almost certainly guilty of peculation, employed him and allowed him for a certain time to retain his salary as Master of the Jewel House.

There is at Dogmersfield the following release to Sir Henry :—" We whose names are hereunder written having by Act of Parliament bearing date the 26th day of June last past been constituted and appointed Trustees for the enquiring out, inventoring, and appraising and securing the Goods and Personall Estate of the late King, doe hereby testify and declare that we are fully satisfied that Sir Henry Mildmay K$^{t}$, late Master of the Jewel Office, hath given and delivered unto us a true and full account of all such Goods and Personall Estate of the late King's as were under his trust, and that he hath discovered and offered to our vision all such writings and books of account as any way concern the same. And now are fully confirmed and doe in our conscience believe that he hath dealt honestly and candidly with us.

"And this now attest under our hands
"this first day of January 1649
"PH: CARTERET. J. MEMBRIÈRE.

"A. Mildemay, Jo. V. Belcamp, Henry Groote."

1649 means of course 1650 according to the present system of dating, and the release shows that Sir Henry accounted for what was in his charge ; the next document indicates that he handed over to the Commissioners all that he could.

"15 June 1652. Att the Committee for the sale of the late King's goods. These are to certify all those whom it may concern that Sir Henry Mildmay K$^{t}$; Master of the Jewel House, hath caused to be delivered unto us (according to an Act of Parliament for the sale of the King, Queene, and Princes Goodes) two Crowns called the King and Queene's Crowns, and a third called the Crowne of King Edward the sixth.

"As also the Gold and Silver Plate and divers vessels of Christall and Aggats, belonging as aforesaid, valued distinctly according to such particulars as have been returned by us in a Duplicate or Duplicates to the Council of State, and amounting in whole to above £13,000.

"We certifie likewise that he hath fully satisfied unto the Treasury for the sale of the said Goodes the some of £1801–4–2 for the Plate charged upon him as Master of the aforesaide Office, by Booke, Information, or otherwise, and that we find not on Examination of the Bookes belonging to the said Office that he is chargeable with any more.

"Moreover the said Sir Henry hath by his Deputy searched and caused to be searched the Bookes, Indentures, Charges and Receipts for the Plate delivered for the King's Officers, or to other persons, with what was owing by them in particular, and uppon our request has assisted us by his Deputy in drawing up an account of what may properly be recovered, amounting to a considerable sum.

"The said Sir Henry hath also voluntarily taken his oath before us that there is not to his knowledge any other Booke or Bookes of Charges pertaining to his said Office but what he hath produced before us, and hath further declared :—

"That there is not to his Knowledge and Remembrance any more Plate chargeable uppon himself (as Master of the said Office or any other) by any Record in the said Office to the value of an ounce, but what he hath delivered upp, accounted, discharged, or payd for as aforesaid.

" DAVID POWELL—JOHN HOCHE—GEO WITHER
" RALPH GRATTON—HENRY CREETH—JOHN HUMFREY."

Some idea of what was taken may be gathered from a book of the Jewel Office now at Dogmersfield, showing what was delivered to the trustees on the 14th and 15th of August, 1649, and valued by them.

The various items, including the Crowns of the King, Queen, and Edward VI, were computed to be worth more than £5515, being about £55,000 at the present value of money.

Thomas Carte, in his *History of England*, says that in 1644 "Sir Henry Mildmay and Henry Martin had been employed to view the Regalia in Westminster Abbey, to break open the locks and chests in which they were kept, to set new locks on the doors, and to take an inventory thereof. This visit was followed by another in which Mildmay, conceiving perhaps the prey to belong properly to him as Master of the Jewel Office, first picked out the richest jewels, and then compounded at an easy rate for the remainder ; it can not, without more than Christian charity, be supposed that these men had not then formed the design of destroying the Monarchy of England."

Mr. J. P. Hore, Paleologist, 1 St. John's Park

Mansions, Pembroke Gardens, N., in a letter of 25th January, 1910, states that in the Dutch records he found a great deal of information concerning the English Crown jewels and plate pawned in Holland from 1626 to 1639, and that in the last year mentioned a portion of these National treasures was redeemed for £97,406 16s. 10d., but as the Dutch pawnbrokers made a superclaim for £16,641 9s. 8d. the treasures were withheld until that payment was made, or a decision on the claim given in the Court of Holland. This decision was against the claim and in favour of King Charles I, but Mr. Hore says he has not been able to find proof that the treasures were handed over to England.

Sir Henry was appointed to the Council of State in the Commonwealth on the 13th February, 1648-9, and had to deal with affairs of the Army and Navy, Foreign Trade, Woods and Forests, Public Correspondence, and examination of prisoners. He sat on the trial of Colonel Andrewes, who was tried for High Treason against the Commonwealth, condemned and beheaded, and he had the thanks of the House for his good service in Hampshire at the trial of Captain Burley.

He was nominated with his brother Anthony and others to consider "how the horses and mares belonging to the late King may be so disposed that the breed be not lost."

He advised that the younger children of the

late King should be given into the custody of his brother Anthony, but according to a letter of John Laurans to Secretary Nicholas of 26 January, 1648-9, he had offered for £2000 and Wimbledon to keep the children himself.

One of the most interesting original papers that mentions Sir Henry, and now preserved at Dog-mersfield, is the Order for Arms and Flag from Oliver Cromwell :—

"Gentlemen there has been report made to the Council by Sir Henry Mildmay of your desire to be informed what is to be borne on the flags of those ships that are in the service of the State, and what is to be borne on the stern in lieu of those Arms formerly there engraven.

"The Council resolves that they shall bear the Red Cross only on a White Flag, quite through the Flag, upon the stern the Red Flag in one Escutcheon, and the Harp in the other being the Arms of England and Ireland ; both Escutcheons according to the pattern sent herewith.    The flags to be provided with all expedition for the Summer Guards &c.

"O. CROMWELL

"1648 *Feb*: 23.                          DERBY HOUSE."

The Committee of Hants appealed to Sir Henry on the 19th April, 1649, complaining of the insuffer-able violence and oppressions this County yet laboureth under from the ill-carriage of Colonel Martin's regiment.

K

On the 19th July, 1649, the House of Commons ordered that Sir Henry Mildmay or his Assigns be admitted to come in for the £2000 he was compelled to lend the King before he left the Parliament, for which he has three Tallies and a Privy Seal.

Sir Henry was by way of being a Puritan, and consulted with Peters, the Calvinist, as to the propriety of having prayers every day before the sitting down of the Council.

Lady Mildmay was of a merciful disposition, for in October, 1650, she presented a petition to the House of Commons in favour of Francis Kempe, convicted and condemned for robbing the house of Sir Henry Mildmay, and then in Newgate.   The man was reprieved.

Some histories report Sir Henry to have been ill-pleased with the part he had played, repented of having turned against the King, and to have gradually withdrawn from public life.   On account of his changes of opinion he was known among his contemporaries as Sir Whimsy Mildmay.

Lord Clarendon says, in his *History of the Rebellion*, that Sir Henry Mildmay and Sir John Danvers were the only ones of the Judges known to the King, and writes of them with the greatest scorn and contempt; but Anthony Wood states that there were eight of the Judges whose faces were familiar to the King, and in *Memoirs of Charles I, Warwick, 1702*, one finds :—" By this traitorous and tumultuous Body (the Commons) the King is brought to his Tryall, and removed from Windsor to Sᵗ James', and thence soon brought to Westminster Hall, where he finds a pretended High Court of Justice, consisting of a President one Bradshaw, of Cromwell and most of his chiefe officers, and some of the King's own faithless servants, as Sir Henry Mildmay, Sir John Danvers, the Lord Mounson, and Cornelius Holland (one that had been Clerk of his Kitchen and was then of the Green Cloth), the rest high-flown Parliament men."

On the return of Charles II Sir Henry attempted to escape abroad, but was seized by Lord Winchilsea at Rye, 19 May, 1660, with his servant John Packer and one Jacob Stephens, of Lambeth Marsh, and taken to Dover. Francis Newport, writing to his uncle, Sir Richard Leverson, 29 May, 1660, says:—"I went to see Sir Harry Mildmay in Dover Castle, who denyes to have any share in the judgment of the King, and desires me to try for his pardon ; he is or pretends to be very ill of the stone."

Sir Henry was brought up from Dover to London, 12 June, 1660, tried, and condemned to be drawn on a sledge yearly, on the 27th January, a rope round his neck, to Tyburn and thence to the Tower to be confined for life, and was degraded from his honours and titles.

An account was printed at the time called " The Traytors Pilgrimage from the Tower to Tyburn being a true relation of the drawing of Wᵐ Lord

Mounson, Sir Henry Mildmay, and Squire Wallop, with the manner of the proceedings at Tyburn, in order to the degrading and divesting of them of their former titles and honours, and their declaratory speeches to both the right worshipfull Sheriffs of London and Middlesex."

In the Calendar of the House of Lords there appears :—

" 25 July 1661.   Petition of Sir Henry Mildmay.

"That your pet$^r$ being most deeply sensible of ye just displeasure of ye honb$^{le}$ House of Commons declared against hym and others in the Bill there latelie passed for paines, penalties, and forfeitures, and now depending before your Lopps, the offence therein charged against hym being for sitting and acting in that pretended high Court of Justice for trying and judging of His late Ma$^{te}$ of blessed memory. The onlie end which y$^r$ pet$^r$ proposed to hymselfe for his appearing in that pretended court, was, that hee might by his being there present and observing of their proceedings, bee the better able to improve his utmost care and industry according to his allegeance and special dutie to His late Ma$^{tie}$ to preserve his said Ma$^{ties}$ life, wch y$^r$ pet$^r$ endeavoured with all his diligence, and then also did (as he now doeth) in the sinceritie of his Heart, declare his utter abhorrence and detestacion of that most wicked murther of His late Ma$^{tie}$.

"And inasmuch as the suddeness of y$^r$ pet$^{rs}$ last

appearing before the honb^le House of Commons was such that hee had not then tyme to make proof thereof there of his allegation.

" His most humble prayer therefore to y^r Lopps now is that before the said Bill is passed in y^r Lopps most honble House, y^r pet^r may have liberty to produce his testimony to y^r Lopps for clearing soe much of the integrity of his intentions, wch however it may weigh with y^r good Lopps hee shall humbly submit to your righteous judgment.

"Beseeching y^r Lopps in ye bowels of your compassion to hym and his distressed children to commiserate his sad condition.

" And (as in duty bound) hee shall &c
                              " HENRY MILDMAY."

Annexed :—"Certificate of Dr. E. Warner that Sir Henry Mildmay is suffering from a rupture, and that if the sentence of drawing on a sledge from the Tower to Tyburn were put in execution, it would endanger his life."

His petition was not successful, nor did the doctor's certificate protect him, for Pepys enters 27 January, 1661–2 :—" we met with three sleddes standing there to carry my Lord Mounson, Sir Henry Mildmay, and another to the gallows and back again with ropes round their necks which is to be repeated every year, this being the day of their sentencing the King."

In the report in *State Trials*, 1742, of the trial

of twenty-nine regicides, a Henry Mildmay is
named as one of the jury at the trial of John
Jones, 12 October, 1660, and it is passing strange
that one Henry Mildmay should have sat on the
trial of the King, and another Henry Mildmay on
the trial of one of the regicides, more especially
strange if what Noble says is true, that the Henry
Mildmay who sat on the regicide trial was the son
of Sir Henry one of the King's judges.

Anthony Mildmay's name is given as one of
the witnesses ready to appear at the trial of the
regicides, but he does not seem to have been
called.

In 1662, the Commission under the Great Seal
for the administering an Act for the well-governing
of Corporations, met at the White Hart Inn at
Winchester, and, after electing certain men for
their loyalty, utterly expelled and removed out
of the Corporation Robert Wallop, Sir Henry
Mildmay and others for their disloyalty.

On the 31st March, 16$\frac{6}{4}$4, there was a warrant to
Sir John Robinson to deliver up Henry Mildmay
and others attainted of treason ; another warrant
for their conveyance to Tangiers on board the ship
*Providence*, with a further warrant to the Earl
of Tiveot, Governor of Tangiers, to receive the
said prisoners and keep them in close custody.

Henry Mildmay was allowed out on bail and
permitted to have a servant on account of his
feeble health, and probably he was never put on
board the *Providence*, for he is said to have

SIR HENRY MILDMAY, LYING DEAD ON A BED

gone to Antwerp, and that place could hardly have
been visited on the way to Tangiers. It is asserted
that he died at Antwerp between April, 1644, and
May, 1655, and, according to the *Dictionary of
National Biography*, a friend there had a picture
painted of him to show that at least one of the
regicides had a peaceful end; but family tradition
has it that his servant had the picture painted by
Sir Henry's orders to take to his people in
England.

This curious picture, now at Dogmersfield,
shows him lying dead on a bed, a black cloth
spread over him up to his head, with places cut
out to show his hands and feet.

We have heard it stated that the picture originally
represented a dead body lying on the bed, and that
Jane Lady Mildmay had the black cloth painted
over it, but we have not been able to get this
statement confirmed.

The D.N.B. and all other accounts except one
agree as to his place of death, but Pepys, who ought
to have known, enters 14 May, 1665 :—" I took
coach and to Wanstead where Sir Henry Mildmay
died."

It is probable that Pepys inadvertently wrote
" died " for " lived," for it is not the least likely that
Sir Henry would have been allowed to revisit
Wanstead that had been forfeited to the Crown and
given away.

Nearly all Sir Henry's vast estates were confiscated
but some were saved. Alderman Haliday, by his

will of 1623, directed that the sum of £14,000 should be laid out on the purchase of landed property within 100 miles of London, and devised the same to his daughter Anne, wife of Sir Henry Mildmay, notwithstanding her coverture. The Trustees under the will bought with the money from the ancient family of Seymour the manors of Marwill and Twyford, which included Shawford, near Winchester.

Dame Anne, by deeds of December, 1654, and 22 April, 1656, disposed of all her manors, lands, etc., in Islington and Twyford, leaving them all to her husband for life with remainder to her sons, and thus they escaped forfeiture. Her will of August, 1656, with codicil of February, 1657, disposes of her other real and personal estate. It was proved, April, 1657, by her sister and executrix Dame Margaret Hungerford, and is remarkable for the number of legacies to clergymen.

In this will she desires to be buried in St. Laurence Jewry Church, London, in the grave of her father and mother. This was done, but in a codicil she says :—" Whereas I have at my friend Mr Duckett's four pillars of marble with sockets for them to stand in, black marble streaked with gold, called a bedstead, the same shall be made into a tomb, and if my husband desires to be buried beside me in S. Laurence Old Jewry, our portraiture shall be placed on top, and our six children below."

These latter instructions were not carried out.

In the north vestibule of St. Laurence Jewry Church is a monument with three busts, representing Wm. Haliday, his wife Susanna, and his daughter Anne.

It is of white marble, with some fine sculpture that has been attributed to Grinling Gibbons.

Wanstead Manor was granted to James, Duke of York, and in 1673 was sold to Sir Josiah Child.

Pepys says of the Mildmay house there :—" A fine seat but an old-fashioned house, and being not full of people looks flatly." This house was pulled down in 1715 and a very grand one built near the site, and this again was dismantled in 1824.

# VARIOUS OTHER MILDMAYS FLIT
## ACROSS THE SCENE

SIR WALTER MILDMAY of Pishiobury,
Herts, is said to have purchased that
manor from Queen Elizabeth. He was
the second son of Thomas Mildmay of
Moulsham, who, in his will of 1565, left the
reversion of the manor of Pishoo, Co. Hertford,
between his sons Walter, Henry, and Edward.
Pishoo seems to be what was afterwards called
Pishiobury, and it is probable that Thomas, the
Auditor, bought the manor from Queen Elizabeth,
and not his grandson Walter. At any rate, Walter
lived at Pishiobury in a house built for him by
Inigo Jones, as Horace Walpole records in his
*Anecdotes of Painting,* and remarkable for its " strong
and lofty rooms." (See Salmon's *Hertfordshire.*)

In November, 1604, the manor of Bradwell was
granted to Sir Walter Mildmay and his heirs.

Walter was Sheriff of Herts 1590, when he was
knighted.

Walter married Mary, daughter of Sir Wm.
Waldegrave, and widow of Edward Wyat, left
issue one son, Thomas, who married Anne, daughter
and heir of Dr. Laikes of Sanarden, Kent, and
had two daughters, Mary and Jone, and three sons,

Walter, a barrister, Thomas, and Henry, who married Joane, widow of Thomas Browne.

Thomas sold the Pishiobury estate in 1613 to Lionel Cranfield, possibly to provide portions for his children, of whom no further mention can be found.

Pishiobury was in the parish of Sawbridgeworth, vulgarly Sabsworth, and in the Church of St. Michael in that parish, in a semicircular recess in the north wall, are the effigies of a gentleman and his wife, kneeling in the attitude of prayer upon cushions, opposite to a desk on which a book is lying open ; behind the husband is a son kneeling in the same position. Upon a tablet below the following inscription :—" Hereunder lyeth the bodies of Sir Walter Mildmaye of Sawbridgeworth, K$^{nt}$, and Dame Mary his wife, daughter of Sir W$^m$ Waldegrave of Smallbridge in the Countie of Suffolk, Knight, being the father and mother of Sir Thomas Mildmaye, Knight, their heare apparent, which Sir Walter died 24 February 1606, and Dame Margaret died 2$^d$ of January 1605."

It is to be presumed that Thomas put up this monument to his father and mother, for the inscription calls him Sir Thomas, which he was not till he was knighted in 1609, three years after his father's death, but it is odd that this same inscription refers to Thomas as heir-*apparent* when he must already have succeeded to the paternal estate.

The monument had suffered considerably in the course of time, but was fully restored in 1885 by the Rev. Carew St. John-Mildmay.

In Essex visitations Harl. Soc., vol. xiii., page 122, is stated that Sir Wm. Waldegrave of Smallbroke, married Elizabeth Mildmay who died in 1581. This is no doubt the Sir Wm. Waldegrave mentioned on the memorial tablet to Sir Walter Mildmay, and the latter adds one more to the long list of Mildmays who married their cousins. The mistake of Small*broke* for Small*bridge* is curious.

---

Another Walter Mildmay, a younger son of Thomas Mildmay of Barnes, was seated at Pontlands, Great Waltham, Essex, in the time of James I, and, says the Rev. Hen. Hunter in *London and its Environs :*—" It is a very pleasant village, and inhabited by persons of the greatest respectability." A satisfactory testimonial for this Walter Mildmay.

---

One James Mildmay was in a somewhat humble walk of life, being crier of Gravesend, but he was loyal and suffered for his loyalty, for in July, 1649, the Mayor of Gravesend laid information against him that at the close of his annual proclamation, he owned, contrary to the decree against kingly government, the pretended title of Charles Stuart, son of the late King, and have ordered proceedings to be taken against him, and some other person to be chosen by you for his place.

On the 28th July a warrant was issued to the Keeper of Newgate to receive George Clarke and James Mildmay, committed for treason.

On the 25th August James was taken from Newgate to appear before the Justices of Kent. There is no further record of him, nor is it clear to which branch of the family he belonged, as no one of the name of James can be traced in the pedigree.

William Mildmay of Barnes is mentioned as remarkable for his loyalty to Charles I. There is a portrait of him at Dogmersfield.

John, grandson of John Mildmay of Creatingham, served the Parliament. He was in the Navy, commanded the *Nonsuch* frigate of 150 men and 34 guns in 1650, and on the 17th August assisted in the capture of the *Charity* of Havre de Grace with the French Rear-Admiral on board, when the *Nonsuch* was severely mauled. In Whitelocke's Memorials for 1652 we find :—" Three of them (the Dutch ships) were wholly disabled at the first Brunt, having lost all their masts, and another that was towing off the Rear Admiral was taken by Captain Mildmay in command of the *Nonpareil*." There were forty English ships in this action commanded by Sir George Ayscue against Admiral de Royal with twenty Dutch ships. Again :— " Letters that Captain Mildmay took the *Roebuck* one of the revolted ships with 20 men in her." This ship he afterwards commanded. He also sent French prizes into Poole. He was killed when in command of the *Vanguard* in an action fought with

the Dutch on the 18th, 19th, and 20th February,
1653, between sixty sail of British against eighty
Dutch. On this occasion the *Triumph, Victory,* and
*Vanguard* were engaged with twenty of the enemy.
On the 15th April, 1653, Parliament granted
£1000 to his widow, Ann, half for herself and
half for her children, and in July of that year
she petitioned Parliament for payment of the £500
granted to her children.

———

There was also at this time a Henry Mildmay in
command of the ship *Providence,* possibly the very
ship of that name that was told off to take Sir Henry
Mildmay to Tangiers.

———

Richard Mildmay was admitted as a trooper
to Viscount Conway's troop in Ireland, 27 July,
1644, soon discharged, and employed by his Lordship in Ireland, principally in looking after horses.
He is hardly likely to have been the Richard Mildmay who, according to Harleian MS. 4778, folio 14,
belonged to the Company of Freemasons and was
Warden in 1651.

———

Captain Charles Mildmay of Woodham Mor-
timer, Essex, who was, we believe, a son of Sir
Henry Mildmay of Woodham Walters and Moulsham, was returned in 1660 as having an estate of
£1000 a year, and fit and qualified to be made a
Knight of the Royal Oak, an order that King
Charles II intended to establish for the reward of
those faithful to him.

# CAREW HERVEY MILDMAY OF MARKS

CAREW HERVEY, *alias* Mildmay of Marks Hall, Essex, was the second son of William Mildmay of Barnes, who was the eldest son of Sir Thomas Mildmay of Barnes, and Agnes Winthrop, his wife. William, who died in the lifetime of his father, married 11 June, 1590, Margaret Hervey, coheir to her brother Sir Gawen Hervey, Kt., and the following inscription on Sir George Hervey's monument in Romford Church gives much information :—

"Here lieth Sir George Hervey, K⁵ fourth son of Sir Nicholas Hervey, K⁵ and Dame Bridget his wife, daughter and sole heir of Sir John Wiltshire, K⁵. This Sir George had to wife Dame Frances, daughter and coheir of Sir Leonard Beckwith, K⁵ and of Dame Elizabeth his wife daughter and coheir of Sir Roger Cholmely, K⁵ ; he had by Dame Frances his wife 5 sonnes, whereof 4 buried yong, and the fyft Sir Gawin Hervey, K⁵ married to Mary daughter of Sir Tho Edmonds, K⁵ by whom he hath issue ; and 6 daughters whereof 4 died yong, the fyfte named Margaret married to William Mildemaye, Esquier, sonne and heir apparent of Sir Thomas Mildemaye of Barnes, K⁴ by whom she had 3 sonnes, Thomas, Carew, and Henry."

Sir Gawen Hervey's wife, Mary, died in 1622, and on the death of Sir Gawen himself on the 22nd February, 1626-7, apparently without living issue, the estate of Marks, near Romford, passed to his adopted heir, Carew, the second son of his sister Margaret, who died in 1605, and he was enjoined to take the name of Hervey before or in lieu of that of Mildmay.

The original deed of Sir Gawen Hervey conveying the property to Carew Mildmay, dated 1622, is at Dogmersfield.

Carew Mildmay was born 3 February, 1595-6, and on the 5th May, 1625, was sworn Groom of the King's Jewels and Plate, his cousin Sir Henry Mildmay being Master of the Jewel House, and he is called Carew Hervey, *alias* Mildmay of Marks.

To judge by the papers relating to the Jewel House, still preserved by the family, it would appear that Carew was a more faithful servant of the Crown than Sir Henry, for there are among the papers numerous orders to him from the Trustees of the Commonwealth and from Sir Henry, to deliver up the keys of the Jewel House, and the plate, etc., contained therein, which are endorsed by him :—" Not obeyed."

On the 25th January, 1649, O.S., there is an " Order from the Committee of the Trustees for

the sale of the late King's plate to Colonel Carew
Mildmay to deliver to Thomas Green and
Mr. Meacham all the clocks at Whitehall belong-
ing to the late King.

"GEO: WITHER.—A. MILDEMAY.—JOHN FOOKE.—
M. LEMPRIÈRE."

This is not endorsed.

The following report of the Trustees seems to
make Carew Mildmay somewhat of a Mr. Facing-
both-ways:—

"February 1649. Certificate presented by the
Trustees Somerset House to Parliament that Carew
Mildmay hath served the late King and Parliament
for 25 years last past in the Office of the Jewel
House, the which place was worth unto him for
wages, Liverye, and New Yeares Gifte the sum of
£129–12–0.

"We likewise certify that he hath not received
any money since Michælmas 1640, nor any part of
his wages since Michælmas 1642, so that there is
due unto him at Michælmas 1649, £1047–4–0.

"We likewise certify that we have found in his
custody in the lower Jewel House in gilt and white
plate to the value of £16,496 which is employed in
the use of the State. All which plate we humbly
conceive was by his care and faithfulness preserved,
he staying and faithfully serving the Parliament
when the rest of his fellows deserted and went to
the King.

"All which has made his trust charge, and attend-

L

ance far greater since the beginning of the warre than formerly.

"As for his good affection to and suffering for ye Parliament, we humbly certify that hee from ye beginning freely served ye Parliament in all eminent places of trust in ye country, both civil and military, at his owne charge, readily observing all their orders and commands.

"Lastly we humbly certify that he hath not only preserved the aforesaid Treasury of Plate, but hath by his industry and Paines discovered great quantities of Plate in the hands of others to a considerable value, which may be recovered for the use of the State.

"Jo: Ffoche.—Ralf Grafton.—Hen: Creech.—David Powell.—Jo: Humphrey.—Jo: Belchamp.—H. Mildemay.—J. Lempriere."

Whether Carew Mildmay clung to the Jewel House to serve King or Parliament, or merely to recover the pay due to him, cannot now be determined, but at any rate he did stay there till forcibly turned out.

Eventually he got his pay, or the equivalent of it, for an order of the Council of State of 3 October, 1653, allows Carew Hervey Mildmay 1023oz. of plate in lieu of debt of £1047 4s., but he is ordered to bring to the Council the late King's Great Bible then in his custody.

Even before this he cannot have been very impecunious, for in 1647 the Parliamentary Commissioners sold the mansion house and manors of Greate Greenford and Harwell, Essex, to Carew Mildmay and two others for £3301 10s. 11d.

From the accounts, inventories, memoranda, etc., dealing with the Jewel House, left by Carew Mildmay, we learn with infinite sorrow and regret what splended pieces of goldsmith's work, jewels, art treasures in crystal, agate, etc., were broken up, sold, or dispersed in those troublous times, treasures which at that period were greater than any other country possessed, and which now would be of fabulous value.

The above-quoted report of the Trustees shows that Carew Mildmay served the Parliament in a military capacity. He commanded a Parliamentary regiment, and the Royalists, who naturally regarded him as an enemy, nearly succeeded in capturing him in June, 1648, when a body of the King's horse and foot on their way to Chelmsford attacked Marks, and Carew Mildmay only just saved himself by escaping from one of the windows of the tower and so over the moat. Very shortly after this he took part in the famous siege of Colchester.

At the Restoration he of course found himself in a difficult position, and he promptly sent a petition, May, 1660, to Charles II, in which he humbly prays for restoration to the place of Yeoman of the Jewel House, having served the last two kings therein thirty-six years. Declares he was the only officer left when the King went to York; that he delivered plates and chains to Ambassadors according to warrant; and in 1649 refused entrance to the Trustees for the sale of the late King's goods, who broke open the Office and took plate value £7000, besides what was in the upper Jewel House, where the Crowns and jewels were kept. This petition was referred to the House of Lords 3 August, 1660.

The boldness of the statement that he had served in the Jewel House thirty-six years is remarkable, for this would include the whole period of the Commonwealth, and he possibly made it with a view to claim for back pay.

In another petition he says he only took command of a Parliamentary regiment for the purpose of preserving order, and that he successfully resisted, at the risk of his life, the signing in Essex of the petition for the execution of the King.

He also made a declaration before Sir Harbottle Grimston, the Speaker, that he lays hold of His Majesty's grace and Favour, and will continue His Majesty's loyal and faithful subject.

He must have been adroit in the management of the business, and the petitions and declaration have prove successful, for there is extant a certificate that Carew Hervey Mildmay was Sworn and admitted a Yeoman of the Jewel House 20 July, 1660.

A certificate from Heneage Finch, Solicitor-General, states that Carew Hervey Mildmay is justified in discharge of wages during the Commonwealth.

Colonel Wm. Hawley and Colonel Hercules Low authorised to seize concealed goods belonging to the King, tried to take the plate given to Carew Mildmay by the Commons in 1653 in payment of money due to him. He appealed and petitioned, and the case was settled in his favour by an order of the 7th June, 1667, from the Attorney-General to stay further proceedings in trover for plate against Carew Hervey Mildmay.

He was a magistrate, and there is a report of an examination before him of Robert Hubert, a Frenchman, for throwing fireballs during the fire of London.

Nearly all the family papers of this period or earlier would be worth recording, for there are many besides those referring to the Jewel House. We will quote a few with which we have become acquainted :—

(1) A petition from Sir Walter Raleigh after condemnation.

(2) A list of Her Majesty's ships. 1586
    Men of War of different sizes  .   28
    Others being Merchant Ships of 100
        tons and upwards   .   .   .  135
    Others 40 to 100 tons  .   .   .  656

(3) A list of forts or castles on the *coast* of England. 6 only. Gravesend, Queenboro, Sheerness, *Canterbury*, Margate, Sandwich.

(4) A list of all the Officers of the Court of Revenue, Officers and Ministers of Justice

Keepers of Houses, Parks, Forests, etc., and their fees.

(5) A book of New Year's Gifts to Queen Elizabeth in the 24th year of her reign, Headed—

New Yeres Guiftes geuien to the Quein's Maiestie at her palaice at Westminster by theise persones whose names hereafter enseu.

1st January the yeare abovesaid.

One entry runs :—

A Juell beinge a shippe of golde w[t] sparkes of Diamonds and Rubies all the sailes spred w[t] a worde enameled on them.

A Flower of golde w[t] a faire white rose and iiii small, in the greate rose a small blew sapher and iiii small Rubies, and in the top a colored Dasye w[t] a small lozenged Diamonde in it, a butterflye onder the same w[t] small sparkes of Rubies.

A Flower of goalde w[t] sparkes of Rubies and Diamondes and a hinde sitting upon it w[t] ii small perles pendant.

Item a shakell of golde w[t] thease wordes ' Seviet eternum dulcis quem Torquet Eliza' and a locke of golde hanging at it w[t] a littel chaine of golde.  P O S Z. VI OZ.

(6) 30 June 1600 Grant by Anthony Watson, Bishop of Chichester, to Edward Hext, Esq[re] of felon's goods, viz: those of Nicholas Baker of Somerton Somerset, Yeoman who killed himself, for the benefit of his widow and children.

Carew Mildmay married Dorothy Gerard at St. Giles in the Fields, 25 September, 1626, lived to be near eighty-two, died in 1676, and was buried at Romford. His wife died May, 1667.

Carew was succeeded at Marks by his son Francis, who was appointed Groom of the Jewel Office 19 October, 1660, and discharged from that office in 1662.

"Certificate of the appt of Mr. Francis Hervey, alias Mildmay, to be Groom of the Jewel Office.

"These are to certify all whom it may concern, That by virtue of a warrant directed to me by the Right Honorable Edward, Earl of Manchester, Lord Chamberlain of his Majestie's most honorable Household, I have sworn and admitted Francis Hervey, alias Mildmay, Gent: to be Groom of the Jewel House in ordinary to his Majestie, To receive and enjoy all the Fees, Dues, Rights, and Allowances belonging to that Place in as full and ample manner as any have enjoyed it formerly.

"In witness whereoff I have subscribed these presents at Whitehall this 19th day of October 1660.

"JO: AYTON."

His release now at Dogmersfield runs thus :—

"To all Christian people to whom this wrighting shall come, know yee that I Sir Gilbert Talbott, Kt. Master and Treasurer of His Matie Jewells and Plate, have examined the account of the said Jewell

House, upon the surrender of Mʳ Fran: Hervey, als Mildmay, one of the officers of the said office, to Mʳ Thos Tindall, and not finding any charge therein upon the said Mʳ Fras Hervey als Mildmay, I doe hereby acquitt, exonerate, and discharge the said Fras Hervey als Mildmay his heires, from all accounts, reckonings and charge touching any Jewells, Plate, or Mony belonging to my charge in the said office.   In witness I have hereunto set my hand and seale this fifth day of December in the yeare of Our Lord God, 1662.

"G. TALBOT [Seal.]"

Francis was born in 1630, and married, on the 14th September, 1656, Mathew Honywood only child of Mathew Honywood. She was a posthumous child, and it is said that her father being convinced that the expected infant would be a boy, left his property to Mathew Honywood and the girl who was born received in consequence the name of Mathew.

She had a vast number of relations, for she was great granddaughter of Mrs. Mary Honywood of Marks, who died in her 93rd year in 1620, and who had 16 children, 114 grandchildren, 228 great grandchildren, and fourth generation 9.  Total, 307.

The Honywood family lived at the Marks Hall, two miles from Great Coggeshall, where was a portrait of Mrs. Mary Honywood.

Mrs. Francis Mildmay inherited largely from her uncle, Peter Honeywood, much of her property to pass from her to her son, his great-nephew, also called Mathew.

This son died at York Fort, Bencoolen, west coast of Sumatra, in 1699, and the last clause of his will desires that his slave boy, Alexander, may be sent home to his mother. A lady in Essex must have found him an inconvenient person to take care of.

Others of the family were in the East. Richard, a nephew of Mathew, writes home from Bombay, 24 November, 1718, to his brother Humphrey, and sends him a "Goa stone." This was a ball compounded of drugs and valued as a remedy for, or preventive of, fevers.

William Mildmay was Chief of Surat in 1803. There is an Indian ink drawing of him in the Dogmersfield scrap-book, taken from a picture that was at Moulsham, but which has disappeared.

Francis Hervey Mildmay died in 1703, aged seventy-three. There is a picture of him at Dogmersfield. His wife, Mathew, died March, 1717, æt. seventy-eight. The next in succession at Marks was Francis's eldest son, Carew, who was educated at Emmanuel College, Cambridge, and had trouble there with the authorities about his rooms, which were probably in the Mildmay wing.

A letter from his father of 1677 says :—

"CAREW

"I received your letter, and I am troubled to hear you have beene ill of the Tooth Ake, the weather is cold and wett and you have got some cold by leaving off some cloaths or by wett on your Feete wearing too thin shoes, wch is the worst thing you can doe. I hope by this time your right is granted to you ; and that M^r Duckett seese his error, let not these troubles disquiet, observe what directions I gave you, if you should not, (wch I thinke is out of question) have your right granted to you, part not with your chamber till you have tyme given you to send me word of it. Keep your tankard part not with that, nor let the Colledge Armes be putt on it till my order, for if they turne you out of the Chamber they shall out of the Colledge and the Tankard they shall not have, nor any favour I can hinder them off, discourse you little of the busyness but leave all to M^r Lee to whom present my service, take care of yourselfe, wch with my blessing is all at present from

"Your truly loving Father

"HERVEY als MILDMAY.

" God be thanked we are all well.

" Endorsed : These

" For M^r Carew Mildmay

" Att his Chamber in Emmanuel Colledge, in Cambridge."

Carew married, 17 April, 1688, Anne, daughter of Richard Barrett Lennard of Belhus, Essex. According to the *Hist. of the Barrett and Lennard Families*, Carew married Anne when she was turned out of the house by her father, but the History does not give the reason for such treatment.

Richard Barrett, writing to a friend in 1714, says:—" I can not but tell you I saw old Mildmay at S^t James' in a red coat which provoked laughter."

Carew was only fifty-six in 1714, and need hardly have been described as old.

Carew was Verderer of Epping Forest, owner of Marks for forty years, inherited the Hazlegrove property by will of his cousin Humphrey, died 2 May, 1743, aged eighty-five, and was the last of the Mildmays to be buried at Romford.

He outlived his wife a long time, for she died in 1718.

Behind some wainscoting at Marks were found some old letters, amongst them the following one addressed to Mrs. Carew Mildmay (Anne Barrett). Though somewhat long it is given as an example of the epistolary style of the time.

" April 12 (no other date, probably 1713).

" I am very sorry to hear it is still a month before I must hope for the pleasure of my Dearest Cousin's company at Chevening [Chevening belonged to the Barrett Lennards and was sold by Lady Dacre] for I impatiently long for that happiness and of late have much wanted your advice. Lord Sussex and the good K^t comeing hither on Monday last who did not feel [illegible] his son's interest and giveing me all the assurance he could of the young gentleman's love ; his proposal to me

is very handsome, that iff I have £3000, he will
add so much more to it, and the interest of both
be my jointure, that I shall have power at my death
of disposing of £1000 of that money, and whatever else my Lady may leave me hereafter.  This
I have all the reason that can be to be satisfied with,
for iff I have noe children, I will be glad to have it
in my power to oblige his.  As for proposals for
care of children 'twas at large, that he would what
he was able, but my Lady not being content with
that urged something certain, that if he received
the [illegible] of my portion and ye addition, that
he would settle at his death £3000.  This he said
he could not tell whether he could doe or not, but
would discourse it with his son.  At his going
away he was earnest with me to yield in the point
but I referred all matters of that sort to my Lady
and my friends, and believe Sir Charles so just and
good that I might safely rely upon his word, were
it Prudence soe to do, but where there is soe many
children (though they are provided for) they may
think a settlement upon any of mine more [illegible]
hereafter than now, therefore I can't but desire
something.  At Sir Charles' going away he asked
leave for his son to come and speak for himself to
which my Lady has consented, soe that if he and I
can agree, 'tis possible I may leave Chevening,
which I can never doe without a great deal of
regret.  My Lady's kindness and bounty to me
have ever been very great, and particularly now in
giving the £1000, a favour I never expected, and

indeed have been very much obliged to my good Lord Sussex who employed all his interest with my Lady very successfully in the business. Sir Charles professes great kindness for me, and told me his son need not love me better than he did, therefore iff I doe go into his family may I be soe happy to keep it by my endeavours to pay him that duty, respect, and kindness he will deserve, but my dear Cousin I have that diffidence of myself to feare I shall never bring that happiness they promise themselves. I dont heare the young gentleman is yet come into England, but his father expected him every day. About a fortnight since I acquainted my brother Edward that the match was [illegible] for answer he told me amongst an abundance of other things how much a greater prospect of happiness there was when the man I married began his altered state at the same time, and had not anybody to share his affection with me, and mine by him, but concluded all with hearty prayers and good wishes &c. He is now gone into Gloucestershire and about Whitsuntide talks of being here with my sister. As soon as I can I shall acquaint him with the Proposall, desiring the approval of my Friends in whatever I doe. The civil visit you received from my cousin Barrett amazes us all, and I wish if it be in order to matrimony it may likewise be to beginning a strong reformation of his life. The widow is very pretty, and I believe good too, therefore without he be better, I can not wish he had her.

" My Lady is very well, gives her service to you, with abundance of blessings to you and your little one, not forgetting [illegible].    My Brother and Sister are your humble Servants, and all joyn in wishing you a good going abroad.    Poor Mademoiselle grieves she can't tell how to accept your offer towards the conveyance of her person to Marks now, but believes she may hereafter, and at present hopes before itt be long to see you as does

" Your most constant

" Affectionate humble servant

" E. CHUTE.

" My humblest service to my dear Cousin Lennard, and my Cousin Mildmay.

" To the Honored

" Mrs ANNE MILDMAY

" Att Marks

" Near Romford, Essex."

Truly Mistress E. Chute was not a lady who intended to marry in haste and repent at leisure.

# CAREW H. MILDMAY OF MARKS AND HAZLEGROVE

CAREW HERVEY MILDMAY and Anne Barrett had two daughters—Anne, married to Thomas Saville ; she died in 1765 and was buried at St. Laurence Jewry, London, and Editha, who never married. Also three sons—Carew Hervey, Humphrey, and Richard, who died in 1719 at Bombay. The eldest, Carew Hervey, was born in 1690, and succeeded to the Marks and Queen Camel, or as it came to be called the Hazlegrove, estates. He divided his time between them, and spent some months of the year at each place. Being very strong and energetic all through his long life, he used to go to and from Marks to London or Queen Camel in the family coach and six.

For some time he was Member of Parliament for Harwich, and when a young man was private secretary to Henry St John, Viscount Bolingbroke. On one occasion when Mildmay waited on him to know when he would be wanted, Lord Bolingbroke named a day, then called him back and said :—" By the bye I shall be drunk on that day, you had better come the next."

Carew was fond of society, and being gifted as a

dancer was once selected to dance a minuet before Queen Anne.

Horace Walpole, in a letter to George Montagu dated 5 April, 1765, says :—"Mr. Chute has quitted his bed today the first time for above five weeks, but is still swathed like a mummy. He was near relapsing, for old Mildmay, whose lungs, and memory, and tongue will never wear out, talked to him the other night from eight till half an hour after ten on the poor bill, but he has been more comfortable with Lord Dacre and me this evening."

The old gentleman, always hospitable, was very fond of entertaining, and in *Memories of Old Rumford* it is recorded that "John Tyler who died aged 90 in 1858 used to say that when he was residing at Pigtails he often saw as many as six coaches coming from Marks on a Sunday morning bringing to Rumford Church old Carew Mildmay and his numerous guests." The same work quotes from a letter dated 12 September, 1775, from General Oglethorpe to Dr. Geo. Scott, in which the old General says :—"We are to dine by invitation at Mr. Mildmay's on Thursday and see old England, for Marks is what England was three hundred years ago, and well worthy the contemplation of an antiquarian."

The description of Marks as given in *Memories* is well worth transcribing. "The fine quadrangular mansion, of which a view is given in Lysons and another by Prout, was most likely the work of Urswick. Its style was intended more for defence

MARKS HALL, ESSEX

than ornament. Its deep moat with the drawbridge, its two brick battlemented towers, its small windows, its secret ways and hiding places in the floor, were characteristic of a structure such as would be erected in the times in which the lot of Sir Thomas Urswick was cast.

"The old mansion which [the Mildmays] occupied for 160 years, and which stood through the Wars of the Roses, was soon to go. It was regarded with superstitious awe by the peasantry in the neighbourhood, who talked about the mysterious underground passages haunted with ghostly apparitions. These were all put to rout in 1808, when the old house was taken down and the materials dispersed. The very ground on which the mansion stood is now a stackyard. There are only traces of the moat, the walled gardens, and the bowling green. Some of the more important out-buildings remain, and the old kennel which once housed Sir Gawen Hervey's beagles, bequeathed to Bishop Harslett, exists as a ruined cottage. The very name of Marks has passed away and is forgotten, and the once Lordly domain is now only known as the Warren farm."

"Charles Dickens once told a friend that he took Marks Hall, then in ruins, for the scene of the fire in Mr. Haredale's house in Barnaby Rudge, which novel he wrote while staying in the neighbourhood." —(See *Hist. of Barrett and Lennard Families*, page 491.)

Marks estate was sold to the Crown in 1854.

M

Carew Hervey Mildmay was apparently equally fond of Marks and Hazlegrove. At the latter place he built the present house, a small portion of the old one being retained. He was aided in the building by the advice of his brother Humphrey, a man evidently of artistic powers as his letters from Italy show, and the house was designed from one in the Strada Nuova, Genoa. There is one room in the house with some grand carving, believed to be the work of Grinling Gibbons. This was brought from an old manor-house called Ham, standing on a small neighbouring property, sold by Captain Hervey St. John-Mildmay. Another room at Hazlegrove, with an ornamental ceiling, is called Queen Bess's parlour.

Under the original deed of purchase of Queen Camel the landholders were exempt from certain duties, and Carew Mildmay claimed under it exemption from service on county Juries of Servers. His claim was allowed.

On the 8th January, 1742-3, a ship, name unknown, of fifty tons burthen, with no living soul on board, drove on shore at Ringstead, near Weymouth, Dorset, and there were recovered from her eighty-six hogsheads of French wine, a parcel of rosin, and some corks. All this, besides tackle and furniture, Carew Mildmay claimed as flotsam and jetsam, he being lord of the Manor of Upton, in which Ringstead is situate, by right of his wife, Dorothy Eastmont, sole heiress to her father, John Eastmont, who conveyed the manor to her, and his claim was allowed by an order from the Custom House, London, 21 May, 1743, signed by William Wood, Secretary to the Custom House.

Carew Hervey Mildmay died 18 January, 1784, and was buried in Sherborne Minster; his fine monument there formerly stood in the chancel, but is now in the vestry.

By his first wife, Dorothy Eastmont of Sherborne, he had four sons and one daughter; only the daughter, Anne, survived him. By his second wife, Edith, daughter of Sir Edward Phelips of Montacute, whom he married 17 May, 1744, he did not have any children.

Carew's will, dated 14 July, 1788, left everything to his daughter Anne and her heirs; failing them to Sir William Mildmay of Moulsham and his heirs; failing them to the three daughters of Carew Mildmay of Shawford—Jane, Anne, and Letitia in succession in seniority and their heirs; and failing them to Henry Mildmay Eaton, son of Henry Eaton of Rainham, Essex, who had married Elizabeth, the only surviving child of George Mildmay and Rebecca Bonham of Dagenham, Essex, which George was the second son of Francis Mildmay and Mathew Honywood.

Jane, eldest daughter of Carew Mildmay, was the eventual heiress.

Her property was increased by the will of Anne Churchill of Dorchester, who left "to my neice Mrs. Dorothy Mildmay all my lands and hereditaments in the Isle of Wight."

Dorothy was Carew Mildmay's first wife, and the property is still owned by the family.

A sort of diary at Montacute refers unkindly to Mr. Carew Mildmay :—

"The 12 August this year 1772 was remarkable for the death of my Aunt Mildmay at Hazlegrove, who was so kind as to leave me in money and estate to the value of £20,000, beside the reversion of the house and goods in London of Mr. Mildmay, who very scandalously neglected it, sufficient to run into great disrepair and ruin to my great loss afterwards when I became possessed of it at his death in January 1784.

"On the 18th January 1784 died my uncle-in-law Mr. Mildmay disappointing many but not me, although I am of opinion that he not only acted by me and mine meanly but unjustly.

"25th April my wife went to London sold my Aunt Mildmay's house, and sent down to Montacute most of the best of the furniture."

Pennant, in his *London*, 3rd ed., 1793, page 126, says :—"The late Carew Mildmay who after a very long life died a few years ago, used to say that he remembered killing a woodcock on the site of Conduit Street, at that time an open country. He and General Oglethorpe were great intimates and nearly of the same age, and often brought proofs to each other of the length of their recollections."

*Gentleman's Magazine* obituary of 16 January, 1784 :—

CAREW HERVEY MILDMAY, OF MARKS AND HAZLEGROVE

"At Hazlegrove, C. H. Mildway [*sic*] Esqre, in his 94th year. This extraordinary person was one of the representatives of Harwich in the beginning of the present century, and was supposed to be the only remaining Member of Queen Anne's Parliament. He spent the earlier part of his life at the Court of Hanover, and was a particular favorite of the Princess Sophia. On his return to England such was the reputation of his extensive abilities that his acquaintance was sought by all the great men of the age. He was the much esteemed friend of Lord Bolingbroke, and was intimately connected with Lord Bathurst, Sir W. Wyndham, Pope, Addison, &c. He had a principal hand in composing the Guardian, Craftsman, and other periodical papers of that time. Of so singular a turn of mind was he that although he was often pressed to accept the greatest civil offices he constantly refused. He retained all his faculties to the last and could even read the smallest print without the aid of glasses."

Carew Hervey Mildmay is said to have been the last of the Mildmays in the male line.

Certainly he was the last so far as is at present known, but it would not be surprising if another Mildmay was discovered, considering how many members of the family there were at different periods, recorded as having married and had children, the subsequent history of those children remaining unknown.

# THE FITZWALTERS

WE must now go back somewhat in date and record the short-lived Mildmay Peerage, which came into the family through the female line, at least as far as the Barony is concerned.

Sir Thomas Mildmay of Moulsham married, as previously stated, Lady Frances Radcliff, daughter of Henry, Earl of Sussex, and in consequence of that marriage his great grandson Benjamin was summoned to the House of Peers 14 February, 1669–70, as Benjamin Mildmay de Fitzwalter, Chevalier, Baron Fitzwalter, the Radcliff family being extinct in the male line, and the Barony descending in the female. His place of precedence was as the last Baron of Edward I.

Benjamin's grandfather, Sir Henry Mildmay, had previously claimed the Barony, as related by Sir John Bramston in his Autobiography, page 121 :—
"The title of Lord Fitzwalter came to the Mildmays by a marriage very collaterall at the time of intermarriage and for which the grandfather Sir Henry Mildmay had a great contest in the House of Lords in the Parliament that began 3 November 1640, but being poore and a prisoner in the Fleete for debt could not prevail, Sir Thomas Cheeke

who claimed from another daughter of another Earl of Sussex making strong opposition against him."

The petition for the Barony is wrongly accredited in the D. N. B. to Sir Henry Mildmay of the Jewel House, who was not in the line of descent from the house of Radcliff.

Sir Henry, the claimant, was cousin of the half blood to Robert, Earl of Sussex, and Cheek, who opposed him, was cousin of the whole blood to Edward, the last Earl from whom he inherited, and he claimed that the Fitzwalter Barony was a Barony tenure and ought to go with the land, but the Council decided that Barony by tenure had been discontinued for many ages and could not be revived.

It is strange that Sir Henry Mildmay should have been so poor, for he owned house and property in Woodham Walter, and had become heir to his brother, Sir Thomas Mildmay of Moulsham. Perhaps the expense of the visit of Queen Marie de' Medici to Moulsham in 1639 disordered his finances, or perhaps he was addicted to gambling or riotous living. He may have been in the Fleet as early as 1640, but he was certainly arrested for debt and confined there in 1646.

His title seems to have gained partial recognition, for letters of administration of the estate of Sir Henry Appleton, son of Sir Roger Appleton, who married Ann, daughter of Sir Thomas Mildmay of Moulsham, were granted to " Sir Henry

Mildmay, Knight, Baron Fitzwalter," the principal creditor.

His grandson Benjamin, Baron Fitzwalter, married 6 December, 1866, at St. Botolph's, Bishopsgate, Catherine, daughter of John, Lord Fairfax. She died 20 March, 1725, æt. seventy-nine.

Benjamin inherited the Overton estate, Northamptonshire, from his father Robert, which he sold, and died 1 June, 1679, leaving two sons—Charles, who married Elizabeth, daughter of Charles Bertie, and died in 1728 without issue; and Benjamin, who married Frederica, widow of the Earl of Holdernesse, and daughter of Meinhardt, Duke of Schomberg, son of the great Duke.

There are two references to this marriage in the letters of Lady Mary Wortley Montagu:—

"London, 7 Dec: 1723.—But I own at present I am so much out of humour with the actions of Lady Holdernesse, that I never was so heartily ashamed of my petticoats before. You know I suppose that by this discreet match she renounces the care of her children, and I am laughed at by all my acquaintances for my faith in her honour and understanding. My only refuge is the sincere hope that she is out of her senses, and taking herself for the Queen of Sheba and Mr. Mildmay for King Solomon."

"Feb: 1724. Could one believe that Lady Holdernesse is a beauty and in love? She is tenderly attached to the polite Mr. Mildmay and sunk in all the joys of happy love, notwithstanding

BENJAMIN MILDMAY, EARL FITZWALTER

she wants the use of her two hands by a rheumatism, and he has an arm he cannot move. I wish I could send you the particulars of the amour which seems to me as curious as that between two oysters and as well worth the serious enquiry of the naturalists."

On the death of Charles, his brother Benjamin succeeded to the Barony, and was created Earl Fitzwalter and Viscount Harwich 14 May, 1730. He was Lord-Lieutenant of Essex between 1730 and 1750, and served several offices of State, being a Privy Councillor, First Lord of Trade, 1735, Treasurer of the Household, 1737, and was Ambassador in Paris. In the last-named capacity he became possessed of a service of plate still in use on State occasions at Dogmersfield.

Dean Swift did not have a high opinion of the future Earl. In his letters, ed. 1801, there is one to Lord Carteret, 10 May, 1728, in which he writes:—

"The great Duke of Schomberg is buried under the Altar of my Cathedral. My Lady Holdernesse is my old acquaintance, and I writ to her about a small sum to make a monument for her grandfather. I writ to her myself and there was a letter from the Dean and Chapter to desire she would order a monument to be raised to him in my Cathedral. It seems Mildmay, now Lord Fitzwalter, her husband, is a covetous fellow, or whatever the reason we have had no answer. I desire you will tell Lord Fitzwalter that if he will not send fifty pounds to make a monument for the old

Duke, I and the Chapter will erect a small one of ourselves for ten pounds, whereon it shall be expressed that the posterity of the Duke, naming particularly Lady Holdernesse and Mr. Mildmay, not having the generosity to erect a monument we have it done it ourselves. And if for an excuse they pretend they will send for the body, let them know it is mine, and rather than send it I will take up the bones and make of it a skeleton, and put it in my registry office to be a memorial of their baseness to all posterity. This I expect Your Excellency will tell Mr. Mildmay, or as you now call him, Lord Fitzwalter, and I expect likewise that you will let Sir Conyers d'Arcy know how ill I take his neglect in this matter, although to do him justice he averred that Mildmay was so avaricious a wretch that he would let his own father be buried without a coffin to save charges."

The Dean did not succeed in getting Lady Fitzwalter to put up a monument to her grandfather, as may be learnt from the memorial tablet to the great Duke in St. Patrick's Cathedral, but if the above estimate of the Earl is a correct one he was an exception to Mildmays in general, for they have ever belonged rather to the spendthrifts than the misers.

The Earl pulled down the old Moulsham Hall, built by the Auditor temp. Henry VIII, and erected a large mansion of Italian architecture designed by Signor Leoni, and costing over £70,000. So in this instance he was lavish rather than miserly.

MOULSHAM HALL, ESSEX, AS BUILT BY EARL FITZWALTER

Earl Fitzwalter had one son, Robert Schomberg, who died very young, and when he himself died 29 February, 1756, aged eighty-six, and was buried in Chelmsford Church, he left no issue, and his branch of the family became extinct in the male line, the Moulsham estate being bequeathed to his cousin, Sir William Mildmay.

Mary, the sister of Benjamin the first Baron, married, as previously stated, her cousin, Henry Mildmay of Graces, and they had eleven children, the seven males died young, but the daughters married.

The fourth daughter, Frances, married Christopher Fowler, of London, and had several children. Her third son, Edmund, married and left one daughter the wife of Sir Egerton Brook Bridges, who claimed the Barony of Fitzwalter by descent in the female line, but failed to establish his claim.

At Dogmersfield there is a portrait of Charles Lord Fitzwalter, and full-length pictures of the Earl and his Countess.

At the same place there is also a very curious little picture on panel connected with the Fitzwalters of an early period. It is a small half-length of a nun, and painted on top of the panel is :—" Matilda dau: to Lord Robert Fitzwalter poisoned by King John in the Abbey of Dunmow, Essex, 1213."

In a book entitled :—"The famous History of Robert Fitzwalter | Lord of Woodham | stiled | Marshal of God's Armies in the Barons Wars | with | some account of his fair daughter Matilda

who was poisoned by King John," etc., it is
stated:—"I have read that it [the poisoning] was
done with a poached egg, the salt being poisoned
which was for her sauce. Others say a cup of
poison."

The real fact is supposed to be that as their
patron, Robert Fitzwalter, had sided with the other
barons, the monks fabricated this story to make it
appear that his enmity to the monarch arose from
personal motives and the treatment of his daughter.

Thomas Heywood, the dramatist, 1601, makes
out that Matilda was the Maid Marian of Robin
Hood.

Matilda was a granddaughter of Simon de St.
Lyz, Earl of Northampton, whose deed in the
reign of King Stephen provides the first mention of
a Mildmay.

# SIR WILLIAM MILDMAY OF MOULSHAM

WILLIAM MILDMAY who, by the will of his cousin, Earl Fitzwalter, succeeded to the Moulsham estate, belonged to the Springfield Barnes branch of the family. He was born in 1705, son of William Mildmay, Chief of Surat, by Sarah, daughter of — Wilcox, Judge in the Civil Court. He was at Emmanuel College in 1728, and Commissioner in Paris for settling the limits of Nova Scotia in 1754. He was created Baronet in 1765, in which year he was Sheriff of Essex, and is the only one of the family who has left a printed work of any kind. He was author of *On the method of Elections*, 1743 ; *On the Police of France*, 1763 ; *On the Southern Maritime Provinces of France*, 1764 ; *On the trade of England*, 1765 ; *and the Duty of the Sheriffs of London and Middlesex.*

He also left MS. accounts of travels in France, Italy, England, and Scotland. The discomforts and difficulties of travel abroad must have been very great according to Sir William's narrative, but he hardly ever complains.

He started in August, 1748, after the Peace of

Aix-la-Chapelle, with Sir Richard and Lady Hoare for the South of France.

They hired a private vessel, left Dover at 1 a.m. on high tide, and got off Calais at 11 the next morning, after what he calls an easy and agreeable passage. On account of the state of the tide the vessel did not get into harbour till 2 p.m. He was rather bothered at the Custom House, even his pockets being searched. The party bought two chaises, hired a courier to ride in front and prepare lodgings, and after dining at the Table Royale, began their journey. They travelled by Boulogne, which place was full of English people whom Sir William calls fugitives from justice. Then to Montreuil and Abbeville, finding the country between the two places utterly barren, devoid even of trees and hedges. Abbeville was flourishing on account of the manufacture of fine cloth from Spanish wool. The workers in this manufacture, which held a patent monopoly, had various privileges, such as being exempt from having soldiers quartered on them, having salt at prime cost, beer without paying duty, etc. From Abbeville the travellers went on to Amiens, through Breteuil to St. Just and Chantilly. Sir William greatly admired the castle, particularly the great gallery.—" On the sides of which are the pictures representing all the Battles and Sieges of the Great Prince of Condé with his bust at the other end in marble." The Chantilly inn is the first one he abuses, saying it had dirty rooms and beds swarming with bugs.

From Chantilly the party proceeded by St. Denis to Paris, where they lodged at the Hôtel d'Orleans, in the Faubourg St. Germains. They put off seeing the sights till their return, yet stayed a fortnight, and left Paris 19 September for Fontainebleau, then Nemours and Montargis, which last place Sir William calls an old dirty town with ill-paved streets. Then on to Nevers, travelling the whole day alongside the Loire, on which Sir William saw only a few boats, and remarks to what a much better use such a noble river would be put in a trading country like England. Moulins was the next town, a place remarkable for the manufacture of cutlery, of which Sir William scornfully remarks that if their swords are not sharper than their knives, their armies would be able to do little execution. At Pancaudier, in Beaujolais, the travellers had a very bad reception. "First we were conducted in our chaises into a large Barn filled with horses and mules of voituriers and carriers ; having alighted among these we were led up by the help of·a lantern round some winding stairs like a Church Steeple into a long dismal gallery where at the further end they showed us two or three kind of Hogsties with some straw Matrasses which they told us were for our beds ; to our further comfort they had nothing for us to eat and drink ; They wonder'd when we ask'd for milk, how could we expect any when they had no Goats in their Village, but being inform'd we meant Cow's milk their surprise was yet more increas'd, not having seen such an Animal since they had all been destroyed three years before by the late Distemper. Here we first began to hear and see real Distress arising from Dearness of Provisions and want of Men occasioned by the War; so that after a poor Supper and a worse Night's Lodgings amidst Fleas, Bugs, and all kinds of nastiness, we paid them in the Morning what they ask'd, it being vain to talk of Bills or Reckonings to People that could neither read nor cast Accounts." The journey was continued through Roanne and Tarare to Lyons where they arrived on the 25th September and remained a week.

Sir William says the city as well as Paris has been fully described, so he will not enter into any remarks on the buildings, etc., but he gives an interesting description of the old clock on the Cathedral of St. John with all the working figures, including the Virgin Mary and God the Father. He mentions that the beauty of the colour of Lyons silk is due to the qualities of the waters of the Saone. At Lyons the party engaged a *bateau de poste* for thirteen Louis-d'or to take them down the Rhone to Avignon, the boat being large enough to hold both post-chaises. The first stopping-place was Vienne, where were the ruins of a castle, said by tradition to be the castle of Pontius Pilate to which he retired after passing his unjust sentence on the Saviour. Several places were passed. At one part of the river considerable danger was experienced from the strength of the stream and wind, the numerous islands, and the crazy character of the boat. At Pont St. Esprit the river was abandoned, travelling on it being too risky. The post-chaises were again put upon the road, and the party arrived at Avignon on the 5th October. The town at this time belonged to the Pope, the surrounding country to the King of France, so there were difficulties about bridges, coinage, etc. The travellers moved on to Aix, the place recommended to Sir Richard Hoare for his health, and remained there from the 6th October, 1748, to the 24th April, 1749. They had taken thirty-six days to get from Calais to Aix, not counting the time they spent in Paris and Lyons, rather a difference from the *train rapide* of the present day. There is some interest in the description of what was to be seen at Aix and in the neighbourhood, but the locality is too well known to make extracts from the journal desirable. Sir William derives the name of the place from a Roman general, Sextius, who founded the town for the sake of the medicinal waters there, and called it Aquæ Sextii, abbreviated later into Aix. Sir William's account of the general society is curious. He writes:—"As the Gentry are thus indolent in their Business, so are they in their Pleasures ; for the Country not admitting of rural sports, their sole Amusements is in Cards, and some Gallantries among the Ladies ; Here with the greatest regard for the female sex I am obliged to Say that Cards and Gallants seem likewise the sole Happiness of these provincial Ladies ; I mean the married women

N

of this place, for their Daughters are kept confined
in a Convent till marriageable and afterwards kept
up as close at Home, till they go back to the
Convent again for life, or a Match is proposed, in
which Family Alliances has a greater consideration
than either Lover or Fortune, and when married it
comes to their turn to act as their Mothers did
before 'em.  Thus almost every Wife has her
Lover, who follows her in all her visits, and is at
her elbow at every Assembly; the Husbands
contenting themselves by taking their Revenge in
being the Gallant of some other Lady.  The
Husbands in the meanwhile are very complaisant to
their Wives in all the exterior Marks of Ceremony,
but close and reserved with regard to not allowing
them either Money or Clothes; for however
extravagant the Ladies of Paris may be in the
frequent change of their Dress at each Season of the
year, those at Aix have little variety of New, such
as were made at the Wedding serving them for
Finery all their lives after, with an Allowance of
about 24 Louis d'or a year for Pocket Money.
Ladies of the best Families I was assured had
no more, and with this and what they can save
by Cards and Card Money they are obliged to find
themselves in Dress and Chair Hire.  For as to
Family Affairs of Housekeeping and Domestick
concerns, these are no way the concerns of the
Women of this part of the World, a Cook or
Maitre d'Hotel being kept in the House, who
finds the Family a Dinner or Supper at so much

per Head, so that the Mistress has nothing to do but paint and curl all the Morning, then throws a tarnished Robe over a foul Shift, and dirty Waistcoat, for they wear no stays, employs her Time from Half an Hour after Dinner till 2 o'clock the next Morning at one Assembly, whilst her Husband is doing the same at another."

Sir William admits making the acquaintance of some nice well-bred people, the owner of the house in which the travellers lived being one. He was a judge of a light-hearted disposition, and often entertained his guests with a tune on the bagpipes, of all instruments in the world. There were a certain number of English visitors, one being Lady Ann Hamilton ; and Sir William writes oddly enough :—" Lord Ann having died at Auvergne." Sir William visited Marseilles and Toulon, and gives good descriptions of those towns as they then were. The galley and galley slaves specially interested him. He writes :—" Here [Marseilles] are at present about 15 Galleys containing one with another about 300 slaves each, chain'd down into the Places where they are to row, but let out in different Numbers as they may be wanted to work in the Dockyards. They are allowed only Bread and Water and stand the King one with another about 3 Sols a day ; Several of these Slaves who become so for slender Offences are allowed to keep Shops in little Barracks built all along side of the Port, which 'tis the Perquisite of the Commander of the Galleys to let as also to receive so much a

day for the Liberty; to these they are chain'd
down in the Daytime and at Night must return to
their Galleys.    Others are permitted to walk about
the Town chain'd to one another and a Guard to
attend 'em, and for better security a Turk and a
Christian are always chain'd together as not likely
to agree in their manner of escaping; others are
suffer'd to walk about with an Iron Ring only
round one Leg, but they must have some considerable Person bound in a Bond to be responsible for
their Escapes.    Bands of Musik composed of five
or six chain'd together are permitted to walk about
the Streets playing at every House where Strangers
arrive; all these pay for such Liberties which bring
a considerable Perquisite to the Commanders."

Sir William also describes the prisons, ending
with :—"But those who commanded most our
Compassion were the poor Protestants, many of
them brought from Languedoc, and confin'd here
merely upon account of their Religion."

On his way back from Toulon to Aix, Sir William
went to Hyères, Brignolles, and St. Maximin.    Of
the last place he writes :—"Here we stopped to
see the Cathedral famous for the Regularity of it's
Architecture, and it's fine Altar Piece of Marble,
but more so for it's being the Burial Place of Mary
Magdalen and S$^t$ Maximin the first Bishop she
consecrated after her arrival at Marseilles.    In a
Subterranean Chappell they show as Relicks greatley
adored in these parts, the Arm of S$^t$ Maximin, and
the Head of Mary Magdalen with something like

a Piece of Flesh on the Forehead, which they say
has never putrified, our Saviour having once touched
that part with his Finger. And here is also a kind
of Tomb, being the Figure at length in the manner
as she lay in her Cell whilst she did Pennance at
S⁺ Baume."

After six months' residence at Aix, Sir R. Hoare's
health being restored, the party turned homewards,
starting on the 23rd April and travelling by a
different route, reached Paris on the 16th May,
then went on to Brussels and Spa, and returned to
England via Calais and Dover on the 14th September, having been abroad twelve months and
nineteen days. Sir William ends his journal with :—
" having performed so great a Journey without a
single Accident or Day's Inconvenience from first
to last, God be praised."

Considering the difficulties of locomotion and
discomforts experienced, he cannot be called a discontented traveller.

Sir William's record of his tour in Scotland
contains a quaint description of the people of the
Highlands, unflattering as regards the poorer
classes.

" The Poor Peoples Hutts are very wretched
Houses to live in, as can be seen, and some by the
look you would only imagine fitt to put Cattle in ;
they are made of Clods of Durt, cut into pieces
and dry'd, and then Heap'd upon one another to
make a Wall, then lay across a few Poles for a

Roof, on which they put Tivet, wch is Turf cut off the Mountains and Dry'd, and serves for Thatching; they make no Chimneys in 'em, the poor ones, and only leave a little hole or two for Winddows, so that ye Smoke comes out there and at the Door; but there are Hutts that are better made than these, wch are made of great round Stones lay'd one over the other for the Wall, but they are Roof'd with Tivet too, and they have a hole at the top for a Chimney, and better Winddows; they lye generally upon the Ground on Straw wrapp'd round in their Plads, in the worst part of the Highland, tho' in others the poor Creatures do make themselves a kind of Bed; to be sure there can't possibly be any people so poor as the lower sort of the Highlands, nor live more hardly; they are all under the subjection of their Chiefs, to whom they are perfect Slaves, ready upon any occasion to do whatever they would have 'em, and are very firmly attached to 'em, that were they to order 'em to Murder any person they would immediately do it, and there has been many Instances of such Proofs of their Duty: in a very few Hours time one of these Chiefs can summon upon occasion many Hundred of these people of his Clan, and I have heard my Lord Lovit say in less than three Hours, He could draw together above 500 of his People; they are very numerous all over the Country, and they say it is incredible the vast number of people there amongst the Mountains, wch come down at the Highland

Fairs, &c. They are vastly given to stealing, being used to commit Robberies on their Neighbours, and in the Night a party of 'em will carry off into ye Mountains Herds of Goats, Sheep, Cows, or Horses, steal Poultry or do any Mischief they can, being a Rude, Wild, Quarrelsome People; but the Highland Companys of Soldiers, who are called the Highland Watch are dispersed up and down in the Countrys, and they are to look after these Robbers, and are to endeavour to catch 'em if possible, and whenever any Cattel is lost, the person that has lost 'em always applies to these Highland Watch, and they go in search after 'em, and generally find the Cattel, tho' they don't catch the People that stole 'em, who if they are met with are severely punished; no people could ever be fitt to pursue after these Wretches but High-landers, for a Stranger in the Country cou'd not possibly know the ways through the Mountains where they Hide, nor cou'd they so nimbly go up and down 'em. The Highland Companys are kept in the same regular manner as to their Exercising &c. as our Soldiers are, and the Command of them is generally given to the Scotch, tho' they have some English Officers among 'em; in the moun-tainous parts of the Country they have large Herds of Goats, the poor liveing very much on Goats Milk, and Cheese made from it, and it is all over Scotland thought to be exceeding wholesome, and good for people in any ill state of Health, being a great restorative, and particularly good in Consumptive cases, and after any violent illnesses, and the People of Fashion generally once a year go into the Highlands to drink this Milk, or what they call Goat's Whey. The dress of the poor Woman differs very little from the English, they all wear a Plaid as they call it, wch is a piece of the strip'd Plad, 2 breaths sew'd together and 3 yards long ; this they put upon their Heads, and it falls all over their Shoulders lower than their Waists, and covers a good deal of their Face, and reaches down to their Knees before ; the People of Fashion and Quality have left 'em off in great measure, tho' in an undress, and in a morning, they will wear 'em. Some of 'em have exceeding fine Plaids, of which they have several prices, and as Dear as 10 and 12 shgs a yard, but the Ladys are generally made of silk, and mostly of Scarlett. The poor People's Caps are made of Scotch Cloth, and very much like a short Hood ; as for the Gentry of the Country and ye People of Quality, they Dress as well as any People, and are as Genteel, and at the Assembly at Edinburgh I saw as many clever looking well dressed People as in any Assembly anywhere, and for behaviour they are very polite and well bred ; in their manner and dress they imitate the French, but the Gentlemen in particular, because they are generally sent abroad when they are young."

A letter of Sir William's of 1756 to his cousin, Carew Hervey Mildmay of Marks, shows the apprehensions of the time, for he writes:—"On the Church Tower at Burnham are placed two Dragoons every day to watch and give notice of the French Fleet's arrival."

Sir William Mildmay died at Bath, where he had gone for the recovery of his health, on the 8th August, 1771, and having no issue his branch of the family became extinct.

He married his cousin Anne, daughter of Humphrey Mildmay of Shawford, Hants, and bequeathed to her, who survived him, his estates of Moulsham and Burnham, as well as that of Springfield Barnes, which he had purchased in 1758 from Henry Mildmay. All these estates are in Essex.

Sir William's portrait is at Dogmersfield.

# HENRY MILDMAY OF SHAWFORD

LET us now turn to the Shawford branch of the family.

The property of Marwill Twyford and Shawford, near Winchester, purchased for Anne, daughter of Wm. Haliday and wife of Sir Henry Mildmay, was settled by her on her husband and children by deeds of December, 1654, and April, 1656. She made a will of 2 August, 1656, with codicil of February, 1656-7, disposing of some real and personal estate. Of this will her sister Margaret, married to Sir Edward Hungerford, was the executrix.

Her two sons are specially remembered in the will, but of her four daughters only the second, Anne Margaret, is down for any bequest. The eldest daughter, Susan, is mentioned as a legatee in the will of Susanna Countess of Warwick, dated 1645, the said Countess being Susan's grandmother, for she, when widow of Alderman William Haliday, Anne Lady Mildmay's father, married as his second wife Robert Earl of Warwick, who died 19 April, 1658.

Mary Countess of Warwick, says of Susanna in her autobiography :—" A rich woman, who because she was a citizen was not so much respected in the family, as in my opinion she deserved to, for she was one that assuredly feared God."

Anne Lady Mildmay died in 1656, and as by her will she requested her trustees to allow her husband to live in Twyford Manor-house, he may have done so occasionally till the Restoration. But it is not certain who resided there for the next few years after that event, though it seems probable that Henry, Lady Mildmay's second son, was the occupier, and the reason of his being there may perhaps be discovered in an answer of his elder brother William in a petition presented to the House of Lords.

In this answer William averred that his brother had tricked him, who was not of so deep a nature as to perceive his design, out of his estate on pretence of holding it in trust for him.

Probably money matters between the two brothers were not in a satisfactory state, for 1 June, 1685, there was a petition in the House of Lords from Henry Mildmay and Haliday Mildmay, his only son, to set aside a jointure said to be due to Mary Brewster, widow of his deceased brother William.

Dame Anne, their mother, had devised £6000, and certain leases to trustees for the benefit of William, who was buried at Danbury, where his tombstone inside the church records :—

"Here lyeth interred the bodie | of W^m Mildmay Esqre | eldest son of Sir Henry | Mildmay of Wanstead, K^t | and Dame Anne his wife | one of the daughters and | coheirs of W^m Haliday |

Alderman of London. He dyed June the first 1682 | aged 60 years leaving | his most loving and beloved | wife Mary eldest daughter | of John Brewster of | Wyfield in the parish of | Barking in the County of | Essex, Esqre, his executrix."

It was not till the 20th May, 1615, three years after William's death, that commission was issued to Henry Mildmay, son of Lady Mildmay, late of Wanstead, Co. Essex, to administer the goods, etc., Dame Margaret Hungerford, now being dead, and from that time Henry was in full possession of the Twyford and Newington estates, and such other property as had been by chance saved from the wreck of his father's fortunes. He was, however, rated at Twyford for the relief of the poor from 1677 to 1705.

Henry was Sheriff of Hampshire in 1688, and there was a licence to live out of his county, notwithstanding his office. In his petition for this licence he described himself as a barrister of Gray's Inn, and engaged in concerns in town.

The treatment of the Revolutionary Mildmays cannot be called harsh, for not only was there no molestation of the children of Sir Henry Mildmay, one of the judges of Charles I, but, as above stated, one was made Sheriff of Hampshire ; Carew Mildmay of Marks was reinstated in the Jewel Office ; and Henry Mildmay of Graces, the Commonwealth Colonel, had licence to come to town about his occasions in June, 1670, notwithstanding the late proclamation.

Perhaps Charles, Earl of Warwick, one of the Commissioners sent to invite the return of Charles II, and a relation of the Earl of Warwick, husband of Susanna Haliday, may have acted as a protector of the Mildmay family.

In a MS. book that was once at Shawford, called the President Book, there is the following poem apparently in Henry Mildmay's handwriting, and which may have been composed by him.

" 1679. Dec: 10.

### A SONG OF MORTALLITYE

When I shall leave this clod of clay,
When I shall see that happy day
That a cold tomb, and a winding sheet
Shall end my tears, my grief and fears,
And lay me silent at my conqueror's feet.
  When a dear friend shall say he's gone
  Alasse hath left us all alone
I saw him gasping, and I saw him strive
  In vain amidst his paine
  His eyestrings breaking
  And his falling jaw
Then shall no teares bedew my hearse
  Noe sad uncomfortable verse
  My onlamented death shall have.
Then friends for a while be merry without me
And as fast as you die come flocking about me
In gardens and groves our day reavell we'll keepe
And all night my theorbo shall rock you to sleep
So happy we'll prove that mortals above
Shall envy our musick, shall envy our love."

The little poem may perhaps be best described by one of its own lines as " sad uncomfortable verse."

Henry of Shawford apparently wished to live at Wanstead, for he had a suit-at-law for its recovery, as being settled on his mother, but failed because it did not form part of her paternal estate. He was a man of grand ideas, for Wanstead was a large place, and Twyford Manor-house he found too insignificant, so, according to Lysons, he spent £10,000 in building Shawford House.

He was evidently an extravagant man, often in debt, partly, according to his own account, from the prodigality of his son. A petition of his to the House of Commons of 27 October, 1790, sets forth that Dame Margaret Hungerford devised her copyhold estate at Newington to him, being worth £250 per annum, and he wishes to sell this to pay his debts. Petition granted.

One of the persons from whom he constantly borrowed money was his cousin Francis Hervey Mildmay of Marks, but his great friendship with this cousin did not continue, for on the 10th October, 1702, he writes to him :—" The bad usage of your Lady to the daughter of Mr. Davies my trusty agent and chief officer, hath altered my mind and intention in the settlement of my estate in your family. It was a bad fate in my family that by the misfortune of my father I lost Wanstead, and by a different circumstance your son Carew will be unfortunate in you."

Henry married, 30 August, 1674, Alice, daughter

of Sir Moundsford Brampton, Master of the
Chancery. She died 20 January, 1692, and was
buried at Woodham Walter. They had only one
child, a boy named Haliday. He married Ann
Bawdon, who died in 1698. They had two children,
a son, Charles, who died young, and a daughter,
Letitia, who became a great heiress. Her aunt
Letitia Bawdon tried to take charge of her on the
death of her mother, but this her grandfather
Henry Mildmay would not permit.

Haliday predeceased his father, dying on the 9th
November, 1696, both he and his wife being buried
at Twyford in woollen, according to law.

His father writing about his death to his cousin
Cecilia says :—" He continued hunting in his coach
with his wife and sperrits to support him until 3
dayes before he died, and a Fortnight before made
new and rich Apparell for himself and Liveryes for
his men."

Haliday must have been very young when he
married, for he could have been but little over
twenty-one when he died.

Henry Mildmay was apparently determined that
if possible the bulk of his property should remain
in the family, for he left almost all his manors to
his granddaughter Letitia if she married Humphrey
or Richard, younger sons of Carew Hervey Mildmay of Marks, or failing them, Francis, the youngest
brother of Carew ; and if after marriage she had no
heirs male, the properties to pass to Walter Mildmay,
Rector of Twyford, a brother of Carew of Marks.

The manor of Henstead, Suffolk, Henry Mildmay left to his Haliday relations, in trust for Apphia Haliday, a somewhat unusual Christian name.

Henry died 11 March, 1704–5, was buried in the same vault as his mother in St. Laurence Jewry Church, and could hardly have been in his grave when the will was proved 14 March.

There is a tale, with but scant evidence in support of it, that the two boys, Humphrey and Richard, were brought for Letitia to choose from, and as the wish was that she should marry Humphrey, he was very smartly dressed, and Richard very poorly, her choice naturally falling on the one in smart clothes.

At any rate she did marry Humphrey at Twyford, 20 August, 1706, he being fourteen years of age and she twelve, for she was baptized at Hackney, 7 August, 1694. The children are said to have gone back to their respective schoolrooms directly after marriage.

Carew Hervey Mildmay of Marks was, by will, left guardian of Letitia, and this caused a lawsuit between him and Letitia's grandmother, Lady Bawdon, who claimed the guardianship but did not get it.

The extraordinary early marriage of Humphrey and Letitia was doubtless effected for the purpose of securing the heiress, and it is also extraordinary that it should have taken place in the church, which presumably was the case, for the marriage is recorded without comment in the church registers.

Their first son, Henry, was christened at Twyford,

18 November, 1712; their second son, Carew, 4 November, 1717; and they had two daughters, Anne and Catherine.

Letitia was buried at Twyford, 29 October, 1749, and Humphrey at the same place in 1761; at least there is a stone in the churchyard to his memory.

Walter Mildmay, the Rector, who died 21 September, 1743, is also buried at Twyford. His folio Prayer Book in the old leather binding is still in use at the neighbouring church of Owslebury. On one outside cover is stamped "The Rev$^d$ M$^r$. Walter | Mildmay | Vicar 1721"; and on the other cover, "The gift of the | R$^t$ Honb$^{le}$ The | Lady Alice Carpenter." At the same church there is a fine Communion paten, inscribed:—"This with my Soule I dedicate to God. Alice Mildmay 1680"; and a remarkable chalice called The Owslebury Cup of the date of King Edward VI. Alice, the donor of the paten, was the wife of Henry Mildmay of Shawford.

Henry, the elder son of Humphrey and Letitia, died unmarried in 1734, and was buried at Sherborne. Catherine also did not marry, but Anne married her cousin, Sir William Mildmay of Moulsham, and had no issue.

Carew, the second son of Humphrey and Letitia, married Jane, daughter of William Pescod, Recorder of Winchester. They had three daughters—Jane, Anne, and Letitia, and Jane managed to prevent the disappearance of the name of Mildmay.

It is certainly strange how the once large family

o

of Mildmay managed to dwindle away. In the reign of King Charles I the Mildmays had spread over a great part of Essex, for there were then nine families in that county with considerable estates, viz.: Sir Thomas, Bart., of Moulsham; Sir Henry, Kt., of Wanstead; Sir Thomas, Kt., of Springfield Barnes; Sir Henry, Kt., of Graces; Sir Walter, Kt., of Great Baddow; Sir Robert, Kt., of Terling; Sir Henry, Kt., of Woodham Walter; and Carew Hervey of Marks. The rental of all these estates totalling about £7500 per annum.

As William Playfair grandiloquently puts it:— " The property held by various branches of the Mildmay family in Essex was almost princely, and it may be truly said, whether we look to the extent of their possessions, or the more valuable qualities of head and heart, that the name conferred considerable honour on their native country."

These princely possessions were mainly properties acquired at the time of the dissolution of the monasteries, and some people might be inclined to adopt the theory of Spelman that ownership of lands taken from the Church was fatal, but to endogamy and not sacrilege must we look for the extinction of so many branches of the family.

Marriage after marriage between cousins was the reason why there was often no issue, or, if there were children, why they died in infancy or youth.

# JANE MILDMAY AND HER DESCENDANTS

ALL the three daughters of Carew Mildmay of Shawford and Jane Pescod married.

Letitia, the youngest, married 15 October, 1791, George William Ricketts of Lainstone, Hants, or, as he is designated in the marriage licence, of Bishop's Sutton. She was buried at Twyford 4 April, 1839, aged seventy. Anne, the second daughter, married, 13 November, 1794, John Clerke, Esq., of Worthing, Hants. She was buried at Twyford 27 May, 1820, aged fifty-three. Jane, the eldest, born December, 1764, married, 22 June, 1786, Sir Henry Paulet St. John, Bart., of Dogmersfield Park, Hants, who took the name and arms of Mildmay by Royal Warrant of the 8th December, 1790, the family from that time being known as St. John-Mildmay.

Jane Mildmay became a considerable heiress. On the death of Anne, daughter of Carew Mildmay of Hazlegrove and Marks, in 1789, she succeeded to the estates of Hazlegrove, Somersetshire, returned at 3924 acres, and Marks Hall, Essex, sold to the Crown in 1854; in 1795, on the death

of Anne, widow of Sir William Mildmay, inherited
the estates of Moulsham, Springfield Barnes, and
Burnham, Essex; and in 1799, on the death of
her mother, entered into full possession of the
estate of Shawford, Hants, and the property at
Newington Green, both of these being subsequently
sold.

Dogmersfield Manor, the property of Sir Henry
St. John, called Ornesveldt in Domesday, was
granted in the early part of the twelfth century by
Henry I to Godfrey, Bishop of Bath and Wells,
and called in the charter Dokmeresfeld.  In the
MS. of the Dean and Chapter of Wells the name
is written Dochemerefeld, Dochemeresfelda, Doga-
merefeld, Dokemerefend, Dokmeresfeld, and Doke-
meresfeld, as well as Dokmeresfeld.

Henry II granted to Bishop Reginald leave to
make a park there; Jocelyn Fitz-Jocelyn, Archbishop of Canterbury, translated from Bath and
Wells, died there in 1190; and the fair formerly
held at Dogmersfield was granted by Edward I to
the Bishop of Bath and Wells.

Bishop Lincoln left in his will seven marks for a
mass for the soul of Stephen, Parson of Dokmeresfeld, and the place was evidently a favourite residence of the bishops, for there are numerous
documents of various kinds dated by them from
Dogmersfield.

A brick long preserved at Dogmersfield is believed to have been of the foundation of the
Bishop's Palace, or of the monastery that is sup-

posed to have stood close to the front of the present house.

There were undoubtedly more than one conventual building in the neighbourhood. Part of a nunnery is incorporated with the buildings of a farm near Elvetham. The nun's walk leads from there to the old church at Hartley Row, and the walk is said to be haunted by a nun.

Hartley Wintney nunnery was of the Cistercian order. It is reputed to have been founded in the time of the Conqueror, and contained a prioress and seventeen nuns about the time of the dissolution, when its possessions were valued at £43 3s. per annum or, according to Speed, £59 1s.

A brass in Odiham Church to a Rector of Dogmersfield has a Latin inscription which, translated, states:—" Here lies William Goode, formerly Vicar of Ponteland in Northumbria and Rector of Dogmersfield, who died Sept: XI A.D. 1498, on whose soul God have mercy. Amen."

Catherine of Aragon appears to have passed one night at Dogmersfield, probably in the Bishop's Palace. Miss Strickland mentions this in her *Lives of the Queens of England*, and quotes Leland's *Collectanea* as her authority. Catherine landed at Plymouth on the 2nd October, 1501, and Leland, who gives but meagre information of the stages of her journey, says:—" There his Highness [Henry VII] avaunced himselfe, leavinge the Prince [Arthur] behinde him upon the Plaine, and at the time of ij or iij of the Clocke in the Afternoone,

his Grace entered the Towne of Degmersfield [*sic*]
where the Princesse was arrived ij or iij Houres
before his arriving," &c., and further on, " Uppon
the Morrowe, being the vii day of the Moneth the
Princesse tooke her Journey to Chertsey."

Leland does not give any indication of where
Henry VII was when he " avaunced himselfe " and
left Prince Arthur " on the Plaine," so though one
cannot be quite sure where Degmersfield was, it
in all probability meant Dogmersfield, which in
those days was no doubt a more important place
than it is at present, and having the licence to hold
a fair had also most likely a market, which would
give it the right to be called a town.

A circumstance that tends to prove the former
greater importance of the place is, that in Pilcot
(a hamlet in the parish of Dogmersfield) there is
an old house, now a cottage, which at one time was
evidently a more pretentious place of residence,
and where there was one there may have been
other more important dwellings.

In this old house or cottage the fireplace was
decorated with rather coarsely made Dutch tiles of
the seventeenth century, which have been removed
and stored at Dogmersfield House, and at the top
of one of the windows there is still a strip of old well-
executed coloured glass about $8\frac{1}{4}$ in. $\times 3\frac{1}{2}$ in.    This
shows five quarterings of the family of Killigrew,
and there was no doubt once a larger portion of
coloured glass displaying the coat of arms of
which these were the quarterings.    This glass is

interesting because Thomas Killigrew was surety
at the time of the Restoration for John Mildmay
of Danbury, Essex, Commissioner of Excise. The
connection between the Mildmay and Killigrew
families came from John Mildmay being a son of
Jane Crofts, who married his father, Sir Humphrey
Mildmay, and Thomas Killigrew's wife being a
Crofts of the same family.

Dogmersfield Manor probably reverted to the
Crown at the time of the dissolution of the
monasteries, for it was bestowed by Henry VIII
on the Earl of Southampton, the act being confirmed by Edward VI. Lysons calls it Dog-
mansfield, and it consisted of many copyholds,
freeholds, lands, messuages, and a large tract of
waste, and was sold in 1646 by Thomas, Earl of
Southampton, to one William Godson. In the
reign of Charles II the manor was possessed by
Anthony Bathurst, who afterwards conveyed it to
one Edward Goodyer, whose descendant Martha
inherited the same in 1725, having married,
31 January, 1702-3, as his second wife, Ellis
St. John, Esq., who had been Ellis Mews
and took the name of St. John on account
of his first marriage, which was with his cousin
Frances, sister and heir of Oliver St. John, Esq.,
of Farley, Hants.

The name of St. John is derived from St.
Jean le Thomas, overlooking the bay of Mont
St. Michel.

The most certain starting-point for the St. John

family is a document in the cartulary of Mont
St. Michel, dated 1121, referring to a dispute
between the monks of the abbey and Thomas
St. John and his brothers John and Roger. This
Thomas appears in Oxfordshire in 1111—he was
dead in 1130, and his brother John received his
lands. The third brother, Roger, settled in Sussex,
and as the most important of the three, we take
his pedigree thus :—

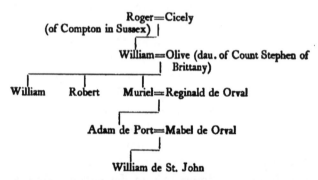

No reason is given in the pedigrees we have seen
why the son of de Port is called de St. John, nor is
the pedigree continued.

The Ports date from Hugh de Port, 1086, of
Basing and Maple Durwell. The Complete Peerage
shows connection between the present St. Johns
of Bletsho and Bolingbroke and Sir Oliver St.
John of Bletsho, 1437. If, as asserted, he descended from the feudal barons of his name, his
own descendants can claim the very rare, if not
unique, distinction of direct descent in the male

line from a great Domesday tenant-in-chief (Hugh
de Port), but this has not been proved, and as
Dr. Horace Round writes :—"It is greatly to be
wished that a pedigree so exceptionally fine should
be placed beyond cavil by the publication of the
proofs."

Ellis St. John was presumably the builder of the
present Dogmersfield house, for the head of a
rainwater pipe on the north front bears the initials
E.S. and the date 1728, and he did not die till
1729. The west front was enlarged, probably in
1744, for that date is on a rainwater pipe on that
front.

The Rev. Carew St. John-Mildmay contests
this, and maintains that part of the old palace of
the bishops was incorporated in the present house,
and considers that if the palace had been completely
destroyed and an entirely new house built, some
tradition of the fact would have been handed
down. No trace of such tradition can be found.

The kennels were once 150 yards from the
north-east front of the house, and the iron hook on
which was hung the meat for the dogs is still to
be seen embedded in a queer old twisted maple.

There have been three Protestant churches at
Dogmersfield. The first one was quite close to
the house, when built we do not know, but it was
pulled down in 1803. The parish registers begin
in 1695 and run almost consecutively to the
present time. The second church was built not
much further off close to the Home Farm. This

was dismantled in 1845, when the present church was erected close to the village and about 1¼ mile from the house.

In the burial ground of this church there is a memorial to "Ann Taplin | formerly Drimes | died 24 March 1865 | in her 102$^d$ year | She was baptized | in Crondale Church | 8 July 1763." Ann Taplin used to state that she could very well remember her christening, being old enough to stand up during the ceremony, and this, if true, would certainly make her more than 102 years old at her death.

The extensive property of Lord Zouche around Odiham was purchased about 1750, out of the Court of Chancery by Sir Paulet St. John, first Baronet, grandfather of Sir Henry St. John-Mildmay, third Baronet.

This property would probably be more valuable if Odiham still returned a Member to Parliament, as was the case in the far past, and if the silk manufacture that flourished there up to a hundred years ago had not died out.

An interesting piece of Mildmay property in Odiham is the Place Gate Farm, a corruption of Palace Gate, for here stood a palace, perhaps belonging to the Crown, perhaps to the Bishop of Winchester, but at any rate visited by Queen Elizabeth, as recorded by Nicholls in his *Progresses*, and tradition has it that the Queen while still Princess Elizabeth was sent here in disgrace for being refractory.

There are still some remains of the palace above-ground forming part of the farm buildings, and to a far greater extent there are remains underground, such as part of a spiral staircase, and vaulted rooms and passages that were probably prisons, for two *oubliettes* were found having no light, and which are now covered over. From the palace there were underground passages, now closed, one leading to the neighbouring priory, and one that came out in the churchyard close to the church.

Dogmersfield House preserves a memento of the confinement of French prisoners at Odiham in the shape of a well-executed model of a French three-masted man of war with a number of guns mounted, the whole made out of bone probably saved by the prisoners from their meat rations.

On the south side of the park wall was a large white mark to which point the French prisoners were allowed to walk from Odiham.

Sir Henry St. John-Mildmay had for a time lands in Norwood Park in the parish of St. John, Glastonbury.

He also inherited Betchworth in Surrey from his aunt, Judith Tucker, in 1794, and sold it in 1798. It may here be noted that the manuscript of *The Light of Nature*, by Abraham Tucker, is at Dogmersfield, far the greater part, if not the whole, being in the handwriting of the author. The 2nd edition of that work, 1805, 7 vols., contains :—
" Some account of the life of the Author by Sir Henry P. S^t John-Mildmay."

Sir Henry and Lady Mildmay had a house in Winchester called Eastgate House, with adjacent grounds. This four-storeyed mansion on the west side of Eastgate Street is depicted under the name of " Mr. Penton's Seat " in Godwin's map of the city published in 1750.

According to the account, most kindly furnished by Mr. Thomas Kirby, Bursar of Winchester College, the house was erected on some part of the site of the dissolved priory of Black Friars, near the east gate of the City of Winchester, granted by Henry VIII to Winchester College in 1544 in exchange for other property. Its annual value at the time was 20s.

The site of the priory, including the prior's lodging, gardens, and graveyard, occupied about 2½ acres, and may be described roughly as bounded by the Broadway on the south, by St. John's Hospital on the west, by a branch of the River Itchen on the north, and by Eastgate Street on the east.

It was the practice of the College to demise the site from time to time on leases of forty years, which were renewed at first every fourteen years, and afterwards every ten years on payment of a fine or premium.

In the reign of Charles II, Sir Robert Mason, who died in 1685, was the College tenant, and built Eastgate House.

The next lessee of importance was Henry Penton, Esq., Mayor of and M.P. for Winchester.

King George III and Queen Charlotte visited him
at Eastgate House on the 28th September, 1778
(having posted from Windsor in 4½ hours), and
held a levee, which was attended by the Warden
and Fellows of the College, the Mayor and
Corporation, and the principal gentry of the neighbourhood.

The next lessee was Sir Henry St. John-Mildmay,
and after his decease in 1808 the lease was renewed
in 1818, 1828, and 1838 to Dame Jane, his widow.

Eastgate House was taken down in 1847, and
shortly afterwards a Mr. John Cave, merchant, of
Winchester, purchased the tenancy of the site, paying £700 down for a lease of forty years at the
ancient accustomed rent of 13s. 4d., 19 gallons of
wheat, and 76 gallons of malt yearly.

In 1869 this lease was surrendered, when the
Lion Brewery and twenty-seven houses were built
on the site.

The description of the premises runs thus :—

"All that their scite of a tenement and garden
with the appurtenances situate lying and being
within the City of Winchester near the East Gate
of the same City wherein Sir Robert Mason heretofore dwelt together with all their scite, circuit, and
precincts of the late dissolved house called the
Black Fryars situate lying and being within the
said City of Winchester with the orchards, gardens,
watercourses, waters, feedings, and all buildings
now erected or to be erected in the said premises

or any of them, and all and singular the appurtenances thereunto belonging and appertaining.
All which were formerly in the tenure or occupation of the said Sir Robert Mason, deceased, and
lately of Sir Henry Paulet St. John-Mildmay,
deceased."

The staircase from Eastgate House is at present
at Abbot's Barton, the residence of Barrow W.
Simmonds, Esq. It is of carved and inlaid oak,
of handsome design, and may be attributed to Sir
Christopher Wren.

According to the list very kindly made for us
by Alderman Stopher of Winchester, the following
members of the family were Freemen of the City
of Winchester :—

Sir Henry Mildmay, Kt., admitted 17 December,
1647.

Carew Mildmay, admitted 29 April, 1750.

Sir H. P. St. John-Mildmay, admitted 2 January,
1798.

H. St. J. C. St. John-Mildmay, admitted 22 October,
1799.

Paulet St. John-Mildmay, admitted 22 October,
1799.

Charles W. St. John-Mildmay, admitted 21 September, 1810.

Sir H. B. P. St. John-Mildmay, admitted 21 September, 1810.

Sir H. P. St. John-Mildmay was Mayor of
Winchester in 1799, and this accounts for his sons

DOGMERSFIELD PARK, HANTS

H. St. John Carew and Paulet being made Freemen at the very youthful ages of eleven and eight
respectively.

## MEMBERS OF PARLIAMENT

### FOR THE CITY OF WINCHESTER

Sir H. P. St. John-Mildmay   .   . 1802–1806
H. St. J. C. St. John-Mildmay .   1807 and 1812
Paulet (called Powlett in list of mem-
   bers of Brooks' Club)   .   . 1818–1837

### FOR HAMPSHIRE

Sir H. P. St. John-Mildmay   .   . 1807–1808

### FOR SOUTHAMPTON

Humphrey  .   .   .   .   1842

Earlier members of Parliament are mentioned in
the various biographical accounts.

Sir Henry and Lady Mildmay had for some
time a house in Cavendish Square, London, and
James Lovelock, who when a lad had been in the
Dogmersfield stables, and who long survived Lady
Mildmay, used to relate how as one of the
postilions, he took her Ladyship in her coach and
four to her house in Cavendish Square, and that they
passed through what he called the snipe ground,
a sort of dismal swamp known as the Five Fields,
where now stands Belgrave Square, and late in life
Lady Mildmay rented No. 30 in that Square.

At six in the morning of the day the family
moved to London a large four-horsed waggon

started with the luggage, got as far as Hounslow
the first day, delivered the baggage the next day
and returned to Hounslow, and came back to
Dogmersfield the third day. Every horse carried
bells, two of them four bells, and two of them
three bells. These are still preserved and hang in
a passage of the house. The old tilt of the waggon
rests on the rafters of the cart-shed. When Sir
Henry and Lady Mildmay returned home the
church bells rang a joyful peal.

A fashionable place Sir Henry and Lady Mildmay patronised was Weymouth, into which town
at the proper season Lady Mildmay, accompanied
by some of her children, drove in her coach and
four with outriders, Sir Henry arriving in equal
state the following day.

After his marriage Sir Henry expended considerable sums on the improvement of Dogmersfield. The large sheet of water in the park called
the Tundry was made by him. A rather smaller
piece of water known as the Lake is in another
part of the park, together about 44 acres of water.
The total acreage of the beautiful rolling, well-
wooded park is about 650 acres, not including the
water, but including the neighbouring woods,
nearly 1000 acres. Formerly there were deer in
the park, for the *Annual Register* of 1763 records
that a man, who was engaged with others in the
slaying of a deer, was accidentally shot and killed.

(For views of Dogmersfield see *Country Life*,
27 April, 1901.)

SIR HENRY P. ST. JOHN-MILDMAY SHOOTING OVER A PIG THAT HAD BEEN TRAINED
TO POINT AND RETRIEVE

*See Daniel's "Rural Sports," 1807, Vol. III.; "Sporting Magazine," Vol. 36, 1810;*
*Blaine's "Rural Sports," p. 792; Bingley's "Memoirs of British Quadrupeds."*

About three miles from the house is a small river now called the Whitewater, formerly the Deepford, on which there are fishing rights for a considerable stretch of water, and the trout-fishing is remarkably good. An old flybook of Humphrey, a son of Sir Henry, has such entries as:—"July 1826, 3 trout 12½ lbs:, 19 June 1827, 8 trout 27 lbs:, August 1827, 7 trout 23 lbs: (hopping moth and grouse):, September 1829, 1 trout 5½ lbs, 1 of 3½:," and other similar entries. We wish that when fishing that excellent water we had been provided with a hopping moth, but without it we have been fortunate enough to kill one fish of 5 lbs., and the present owner has had one of 6 lbs. 10 oz. On the window-sill of the study is traced the outline of a fish of 9 lbs.; this was caught by Edward Mildmay. The fish from this stream are highly esteemed, being generally pink in flesh and very firm, and Jane Lady Mildmay would at times send a few to H.R.H. the Prince of Wales.

Sir Henry St. John-Mildmay being a man of culture and fond of books added largely to the Dogmersfield library in which were many rare, curious, and beautifully illustrated books, several having the book-plate of Charles Mildmay, Lord Fitzwalter, 1701. The most valuable portion of the library was sold by auction by Messrs. Sotheby and Hodge, in April, 1907.

Sir Henry seems to have played his part in organising troops for the defence of the country,

P

for the present writer purchased an interesting medal commemorating this. It is an oval silver medal with loop at top and rope-pattern border. The medal measures $2\frac{1}{16}$ in. $\times$ $1\frac{11}{16}$ in., the border is $\frac{1}{8}$ in. wide, the loop $\frac{3}{4}$ in. $\times$ $\frac{3}{8}$ in. On the obverse: Laurel wreath round outside edge, then "To Colonel Sir H. S$^t$ John Mildmay"; centre: the Mildmay lion; underneath it "For Services." Reverse: "Hampshire Volunteers" round three parts of outside edge; at bottom of oval "Dogmersfield"; centre a group of flags and a cannon lying on the ground; above them "G.R." within a laurel wreath, and underneath "1804."

Official list published by War Office, 1st October, 1804.

### Dogmersfield Cavalry.

Captain H. P. St. John-Mildmay, Bart., 8 August, 1803.

Cornet H. C. St. John-Mildmay, 4 October, 1803.

Sir Henry commanded but is only gazetted as Captain.

Judging by his recorded speeches in Parliament, Sir Henry was a clear and logical speaker. He had occasion in 1807 to vigorously defend in the House the arrangement made with Government concerning Moulsham, in Essex, belonging to his wife.

He said there was a condition requiring his residence at the mansion for three months in every year, and he did so reside there for six or seven

SIR HENRY P. ST. JOHN-MILDMAY
*Romney*

years, till in 1803 it was found necessary to throw up military works within 400 yards of his house. The works were commenced, and what with the multitude employed on them, amounting to 1500 men, and the numbers brought to that part of Essex by the fear of invasion, which then prevailed, the neighbourhood assumed the appearance of an entrenched camp, all his outdoor property became endangered, his family alarmed, and he himself so inconvenienced that he obtained from Government relief by Act from the necessity of residing there, and compensation to be given him for the house and twenty acres of pleasure grounds at the rate of £400 a year. He might mention that about eighty years ago the house had cost £70,000 in building; there were over fourteen rooms on a floor, one being sixty feet long; it was expensively furnished; the estate was worth £11,000 a year; and he would like to know what gentleman would think £400 a year compensation for being turned out of such a place.

Sir Henry eventually got £1,300 for one year, £600 for subsequent years for so long as the land was occupied by His Majesty.

The military works thrown up at Moulsham were part of the Chelmsford lines constructed by J. T. Jones, afterwards a Major-General, and builder of the famous earthworks at Torres Vedras.

Moulsham Hall was never reoccupied and was pulled down in 1816. Most of the pictures were removed to Dogmersfield, and the red cloth hangings with large wide chairs *en suite* from the state bedroom are now in the drawing-room of that house.

The stone Fitzwalter coat of arms from the pediment of Moulsham is now (1907) fixed in the wall of a motor garage at Brentford, owned by Messrs. Johnson. It is twelve feet long and six feet high, the crest missing. All in good condition save the nose of the dexter lion supporter.

### Blazon of the Arms.

Quarterly of six, three and three :—

1. Argent, three lions rampant azure, for Mildmay.
2. Argent, a bend engrailed sable, for Radcliff.
3. Or, a fess between two chevrons gules, for Fitzwalter.
4. Argent, a lion rampant sable, crowned or, a bordure azure, for Burnell.
5. Or, a saltire engrailed sable, for Bottetort.
6. Argent, three bars gules, for Milton.

On inescutcheon quarterly :—

1 and 4, Argent, an inescutcheon sable, over all an escarbuncle, for Schomberg.

2 and 3, gules six escutcheons, 3, 2, and 1, argent, for Schomberg.

### Supporters :—

Dexter, a lion guardant.
Sinister, a lion reguardant.

Motto :—

### Alla Ta Hara.

Sir Henry had trouble over the oyster fishery in the Crouch River that flowed by his wife's estate of Burnham, Essex, to which everyone thought they had a right. In January, 1808, a notice was posted threatening penalties on the Corps of Sea Fencibles if they tumultuously assembled on the Crouch or Burnham River for the purpose of taking away the oysters laid on the grounds of Sir Henry Mildmay. A case was tried 9 March, 1808, at the Essex Assizes. Records of trials in the reigns of Charles I and Charles II were produced, which clearly proved the right (of exclusive oyster fishery) to be vested in the family of the Earls of Sussex, ancestors of the Mildmay family. This same was also proved by other documents, and the jury found a verdict for the Baronet against those persons who maintained that the river in question being an arm of the sea could not belong to the manor of Burnham.

This was undoubtedly right, for an indenture of 20 December, 22 Elizabeth (1580), of Thomas, Earl of Sussex deals with Burnham Manor amongst other property, and after mentioning several heirs, settles the manor on Lady Frances Ratcliff, wife of Sir Thomas Mildmay of Moulsham, and from him it has descended to its present owner, Major Sir H. St. J. Mildmay.

Sir Henry and Lady Mildmay had sixteen children ; they are recorded in a Bible of the date of

1741, that is, at Dogmersfield.  On the cover is stamped " Ellis St. John. 1742."

The children recorded are:—

(1)  Henry St. John Carew (born 16 April, 1787).
(2)  Jane Dorothea.
(3)  Son (lived only one day).
(4 & 5)  Maria and Judith Anne (twins).
(6)  Paulet.
(7)  George William.
(8)  Charles William.
(9)  Humphrey.
(10)  John Francis.
(11)  Edward.
(12)  Walter.
(13)  Carew Anthony.
(14)  Augustus Tucker.
(15)  Letitia.
(16)  Hugo Cornewall (born at Eastgate House).

All the diseases of the children are noted in the Bible, and everyone up to Walter is stated to have had the smallpox, he and the subsequent ones as having the vaccine disease.

The *Observer* of November, 1804, says :—" Sir Henry Mildmay is said to have one of the most interesting families in England.  It consists of ten sons and five daughters, the eldest seventeen and the youngest 12 months.  They are all very handsome and bear a strong resemblance to each other."

A pleasing little notice, but wrong in one point,

TWINS, MARIA AND JUDITH ANNE

for in November, 1804, there were only nine sons, one having died and Hugo not yet born.

The marriages, etc., of all these sons and daughters can easily be learnt from any Baronetage.

As before stated, Henry the eldest, Paulet the third, and Humphrey the sixth son were in Parliament, and Paulet appears in the large picture of the first reformed Parliament, 5 February, 1833, painted by Sir Geo. Hayter, and now in the National Portrait Gallery. Paulet was member for Winchester, and is at the back under the gallery. He previously served in the Army, being gazetted to the Coldstream Guards 14 May, 1807, promoted Lieutenant 3 October, 1811, and retiring in 1812.

"George William" entered the Navy as first-class Volunteer on the *Ardent*, 64, on the 14th September, 1803, and on 28 November was present as Midshipman at the destruction of the French frigate, *La Bayonnaise*, of 32 guns and 300 men. He then served in several ships, became Lieutenant 19 May, 1812, appointed to *Leander*, 50, Captain Sir George Collier, and saw much active service on the coast of America. Later, when in the *Wasp*, 18, he assisted in the capture of the Venezuelan sloop-of-war, *El Libertador*. In 1821 he joined the *Iphigenia*, 42, and in command of the boats of that ship and those of the *Myrmidon* won distinction by the gallant manner in which, overcoming desperate resistance, he effected off the River Bonny the capture of five vessels having on board one thousand eight hundred negroes. For this he was promoted

Commander in 1822. Became Post-Captain in 1828, and from April, 1835, till paid off at the end of 1838, commanded on the home station the *Magicienne*, of 24 guns. While in command of this last ship he took her in a heavy gale of wind, under close-reefed main and fore sails, into the Tagus River, where no other ship of the squadron could manage to follow her. A picture representing this incident is in the possession of his son, the writer of this memoir, who also owns and uses as a counterpane a long blue coverlet, with white design in it, made of native African cotton, and given by the King of Bonny to Lieutenant Mildmay in 1821.

"Humphrey" joined the Coldstream Guards 9 September, 1813; promoted Captain 16 August, 1821; transferred to the 35th Foot 25 December, 1823; and placed on half-pay as Captain 4th February, 1824, from the 95th Regiment, which regiment he never joined. He served for a short time in the Peninsular War, and this is recorded on the tablet erected to his memory. He made one of the few rich marriages of the family when he married in 1823 Anne Eugenia Baring, which gave him an entry into the great Baring house, and in 1828 he was a Governor of the Bank of England.

"John Francis" joined the Navy as first-class Volunteer, 21 April, 1809, served in the *Blake*, *Endymion*, *Antelope*, *Brazen*, *Sybille*, and *Carnation*. Promoted Lieutenant 20 September, 1815, and Commander 25 November, 1822. He was killed

CAPTAIN GEORGE W. ST. JOHN-MILDMAY, R.N.
*D'Orsay*

EDWARD ST. JOHN-MILDMAY

in the streets of Kingston-on-Thames by being thrown out of his gig when in pursuit of another gig. It is sometimes said that he is portrayed in Capt. Marryat's novel, *Frank Mildmay, or the Naval Officer.*

"Edward" was appointed Cornet in the 22nd Light Dragoons, 18 July, 1816, with which regiment he served in India ; promoted Lieutenant 2 October, 1819 ; placed on half-pay 25 September, 1820 ; promoted Captain 2 June, 1825 ; and joined the 10th Foot 8 June, 1826. Retired on half-pay 8 June, 1830.

"Charles William" and "Carew Anthony" were in Holy Orders. The latter was Rector of Chelmsford from 1827 to 1878, and became Archdeacon of Essex. He placed a brass memorial tablet in Chelmsford Church recording the names of forty Mildmays buried there or in the precincts. In 1814, Carew recited in the Sheldonian Theatre, Oxford, his own Greek verses giving an account of a visit of the Prince Regent to the University of Oxford.

The Baronetcy belonged to the St. John family, being granted 9 October, 1772, and Sir Henry P. St. John-Mildmay, who was the third Baronet, died of atrophy in 1808 at the early age of forty-four. Buried at Dogsmerfield, 21 November.

In the *Athenæum* for 1 December, 1808, there is an obituary notice.

"Died, at Bath, aged 44, Sir Henry Paulet St. John-Mildmay of Dagmersfield [*sic*] Park, in

Hampshire, Bart. He was the grandson of Sir
Paulet St. John who was created a Baronet in 1772,
and died in 1780, at the age of 76 :—A downright
country Squire, supposed to be the original from
which Henry Fielding sketched the'Squire Western'
of Tom Jones. His son, Sir Henry St. John, sat
in Parliament for the County, having come in
principally through the interest of the late Duke of
Chandos, who wished to get his interest at Winchester and succeeded. He died in 1784, at the
age of 47, leaving his successor, the late Sir Henry,
an estate heavily encumbered in consequence of the
expensive habits of its former possessors. His son,
Sir Henry, the subject of this article, was born in
1764, and received the rudiments of education
under Mr. Gilpin at Cheam, from whence he was
removed to St. John's College, Cambridge, where
being of quick parts he was esteemed a respectable
scholar. In 1786 he married Jane, eldest daughter
and coheiress of Carew Mildmay of Shawford
House, Esqre. (a granddaughter of his ancestor
Sir Paulet's last wife) and took her family name.
Her fortune was at first moderate, but in consequence of a series of bequests from her family con-
nections he at length became possessed of immense
property. Not less than £20,000 a year. He first
came into Parliament for Westbury in Wiltshire in
1796, but having retrieved the antient family interest
in Winchester, he was returned for that city in 1802
without opposition, and continued to represent it
till the General Election in 1807, when, through

the ministerial influence he was elected a member for Hampshire, and by his death there is now a vacancy in the representation of that county. In parliament (except in one or two instances) he was a steady supporter of the administration, but it has been alleged, that his reason for taking part at all times with the Servants of the Crown, was the ambition of obtaining a seat in the Upper House. Mr. Pitt, though sufficiently profuse of it to others, turned a deaf ear to all his sólicitations for this honour, but the present administration seem to have paid attention to his wishes, for it has lately been reported in the county that he had obtained a promise of being included in the next batch. His public avocations did not occupy the whole of his attention for in 1802 we find him accompanying Mr. Nield in his visits to the various gaols of the metropolis ; and in 1805 he published a second edition in seven vols. 8vo, of 'The Light of Nature Pursued, by Abraham Tucker Esqre,' to which he added 'Some account of the Author,' by himself. He generally resided at Dagmersfield [*sic*] Park, where his establishment was so splendid, and his hospitalities so expensive, that his income, large as it was, could not prevent his being sometimes embarrassed. To the poor in his neighbourhood he frequently made large donations, and by them in particular his loss will be regretted. Besides his eldest son, now Sir Henry Carew Mildmay, one of the members for Winchester, he has left a widow and fourteen children."

As this notice makes no mention of a serious mishap to the subject of it, one may be inclined to doubt the absolute correctness of the statement in the *Annual Register* for December, 1797, that Sir Henry Mildmay attempted to caress a vicious horse named Telegraph that he had been riding, and that the horse instantly seized his right hand in its mouth and crushed it so badly that all the fingers had to be amputated.

There is a fine portrait of Sir Henry, by Romney, at Dogmersfield, for which Sir Henry gave the following sittings: In 1783 nine, in 1784 five, and in 1785 one. The artist was paid £42 for the picture by Sir Henry's aunt, Miss Judith Tucker.

There is also a picture in the Guildhall at Winchester, dated 1808, and labelled Sir Henry Mildmay, but it certainly is not a likeness of him, and probably represents his grandfather Paulet St. John, Esq., once M.P. for Winchester.

Sir Henry was succeeded in the Baronetcy by his eldest son, Henry St. John Carew St. John-Mildmay.

The estates remained mainly in the possession of Jane Lady St. John-Mildmay. Creevy in his *Memoirs*, writing in 1814, mentions a rumour that Jane Lady Mildmay, then a handsome widow, was to marry Lord Folkestone, and her son, Sir Henry, Miss Thayer.

Lord Folkestone later became the husband of Lady Mildmay's daughter, Judith Anne.

JANE, LADY ST. JOHN-MILDMAY, WITH HER SEVENTH SON EDWARD
*By permission of Messrs. P. and D. Colnaghi & Obach*

Lady Mildmay was well-known in society and had many friends among distinguished people. Unfortunately her letters do not seem to have been preserved, and we have been able to discover but four or five not of any great importance.

A letter from King William IV, when Duke of Clarence, refers to her son, John Francis.

" ADMIRALTY, Saturday Night.

" Dear Madam

"In answer to your Ladyship's letter of this day, I can assure the excellent and elegant mother of Commander Mildmay that I shall have sincere pleasure in promoting this young officer the moment I can with propriety, and I ever remain

"Dear Madam, yours most truly

"WILLIAM."

"Excellent and elegant" is a sweetly quaint phrase.

The Rt. Honble. George Canning writes:—

"F.O., Dec. 14, 1825.

" Dear Lady Mildmay

"I am afraid the fates are against our visit to Dogmersfield this year. For first, the King has got a fit of the gout which puts off a Council that was to be held to-morrow, and an audience that was fixed for Friday, for the present indefinitely, but (according to the report of His Majesty's Physicians) in all probability till the middle of next week. I must attend both the Council and the Audience (which is that of one of my Foreign Flock to take leave of the King) and I can not therefore be out of the way till they are over. Secondly (though the first impediment is I fear sufficient) I received yesterday a letter from my son William announcing his arrival at Plymouth from Halifax, where his ship has been pronounced unfit to keep the sea, and he is sent home with his officers and crew to look for another. I do not yet know how the Admiralty mean to dispose of him, nor whether he will be allowed to come up to town, nor when. This last matter I would have tried to manage somehow or other, if the former had not chained me to London. I ought perhaps to have written to you yesterday, but I waited for Friday's report from Windsor in the hope that the attack of gout might pass off—on the contrary it grows worse. I think therefore dear Lady Mildmay it is but fair to release you from any uncertainty about us and to beg you to allow us to defer our visit to a more propitious season.

"Believe me, dear Lady Mildmay

"Very sincerely and faithfully yours

"GEO: CANNING.

"I hope your son is getting better, he is 'a good boy.'"

Canning's fondness for a rhyme is well known. On the occasion of one visit to Dogmersfield, he

said, on arriving at the house, that when driving through the park he noticed a perfectly turned out cart and horse, stopped, and said to the driver:—
" To whom belong that beautiful horse and cart," and the man replied:—" To Sir Henry St. John-Mildmay, Bart."

A letter from the Duke of Wellington of 6 January, 1834, is only an invitation to Lady Mildmay to dine at Strathfieldsaye to meet H.R.H the Duke of Gloucester.

The Rev. Sydney Smith was a very intimate friend of the family, and he writes:—

" *March*, 1845.

" My dear Lady Mildmay

Many thanks for your kind presents of game which I thank you for myself that I may tell you I am better: I have had a very long and severe illness, but am inclined to think I shall get over it. Severe indigestion, breathlessness, and general languor are the evils under which I have suffered, and am now in a lesser degree suffering. Nothing can exceed the skill and kind attention of Dr. Holland. I hope dear Lady Mildmay you are exerting yourself and bearing up bravely against your misfortune, the extent of which nobody can appreciate better than myself. I meant to have proposed myself to you for a day or two this Autumn, but in my present state it is wholly out of the question. I hope you will come to town in the proper season. I think a little variety will do you good.    In me you will find no variety but the same affectionate regard to the end of your days and mine.                    "SYDNEY SMITH."

The misfortune to which reference is made in the above letter may have been the death in the autumn of 1844 of Letitia, Lady Mildmay's youngest daughter, for she was a great favourite of the Rev. Sydney Smith.

In the *Memoirs of Thomas Moore*, vol. iii. page 247, is stated :—" Went to Lady Mildmay for the MS. of Byron I had lent her to read ; sat some time with her.    Mentioned how much she felt afraid of Lord Byron when she used to meet him in society in London ; and that once when he spoke to her in a doorway her heart beat so violently she could hardly answer him.    She said it was not only awe of his great talents but the peculiarity of a sort of tender look he used to give that produced this effect on her."

In Lady Granville's letter, one of the 12th April, 1810, to Lord Hartington, mentions :—" There are shoals of Miss Mildmays and the good-natured Dowager quite like a hen."

Lady Mildmay all through her long life retained in a remarkable degree her mental and bodily vigour.    She never had a serious illness, did not become deaf, or lose her memory or her teeth, and to the last sat upright in an uneasy chair working with her needle, or reading without the aid of spectacles.

JANE, LADY ST. JOHN MILDMAY
*From a sketch by Harlowe*

Her death when over ninety-two years of age may be truly described as "falling asleep." It occurred in London on the 6th May, 1857, and she was buried at Dogmersfield. In 1878 a stained glass east window was placed in St. Mary's Church, Chelmsford, to her memory.

A notice of her death in a Hampshire paper published at Winchester says :—"In our obituary for the present week is recorded the name of the venerable and deeply lamented Dowager Lady Mildmay, whose periodical residence at her mansion in this city, with her family, several years ago, will be remembered, when her hospitalities were for a series of years liberally extended towards her friends, and many of the poorer inhabitants were constant recipients of her unostentatious bounty at Eastgate House. Of this amiable Lady may be truly said, that spared by Divine Providence long beyond the limit allotted to human existence in this world, her whole life, from early maturity, has been one unvaried course of kindness and affection to all the members of her numerous family, and towards the aged, infirm, and necessitous her charities have been unbounded."

A present Alderman of Winchester, 1906, now well advanced in years, told us he well remembered Lady Mildmay driving about the town, calling at the houses of all classes of the community, and that she always remembered every member of a family, asking particularly after each one.

Lady Mildmay's eldest son, Henry St. John

Q

Carew St. John-Mildmay, at the early age of nineteen, was one of Lord Hutchinson's secret mission to Berlin, and General Sir Robert Wilson in his diary records :—" Memel 22 June 1807 arrived at Memel and here found all our old Society increased by Lord Leveson Gower, Mr. Mildmay a son of Sir Henry &c."

On several occasions the General refers to being in Mildmay's company, and Mildmay was evidently well provided, for he took the General in his barouche from Memel to visit friends in the Army.

Disguised in his servant's clothes, he accompanied General Wilson on a dangerous journey towards Tilsit, and afterwards, both dressed as Cossacks by Platow, entered the town to interview Woronzow.

On 15 July Mildmay with several others left Memel for St. Petersburg, after failing in several previous attempts.

Henry Mildmay succeeded to the Baronetcy on the death of his father in 1808, and married, in 1809, Charlotte Bouverie, by whom he had one son.

Lady Granville, in a letter of 12 April, 1810, says :—" Sir Henry and his wife go about in attitudes, but they match so well and look so well that one forgives them for it."

A portrait at Dogmersfield by Sandars of Sir Henry St. John Carew St. John-Mildmay clearly shows the beauty for which, according to the *Observer* of 1804, the family was remarkable.

Still more clearly does this appear in a coloured drawing by Richard Cosway of Sir Henry in fancy dress, now at Hollam.

Sir Henry's handsome wife died in 1810 after one year, less two days, of married life.

Creevy in his *Memoirs* mentions that at a Dandy ball in 1811, the Regent, who was present, sent a message to Sir Henry Mildmay, saying that he wished to speak to him, who replied that it must be a mistake, because His Royal Highness had seen him and taken no notice of him.

Watier's, in Bolton Street, was called the Dandy Club, and Jesse in his *Life of Beau Brummell* says that Lord Byron spoke of Lord Alvanley, Brummell, Sir Henry Mildmay, and Mr. Pierpoint, as the four chiefs. Jesse relates that these four gentlemen gave a fancy ball in July, 1813. The Prince of Wales had quarrelled with Brummell and Sir Henry Mildmay, but after considerable discussion he was invited to the ball by all four gentlemen. On arriving, he showed the feeling he still entertained by making a stately bow to Lord Alvanley and Mr. Pierpoint, and taking no notice whatever of Brummell or Sir Henry Mildmay.

Evidently the Prince of Wales and Sir Henry Mildmay could not agree.

In the *History of White's Club* there appears amongst the recorded bets :—

"Dec: 12, 1812. Sir Henry Mildmay bets M^r Brodrick 100 Guineas to ten that Bonaparte returns to Paris as Emperor.

"Sir Henry Mildmay bets General Grosvenor 100 Guineas to ten that Bonaparte gets safe back to Paris during or at the close of the Russian campaign."

In 1815 Sir Henry married at Wurtemberg his deceased wife's sister, Harriet, and by her had three sons—Edmond, Horace, and Augustus Fitzwalter. She died aged thirty-four, on the 9th December, 1834, and was buried at Milan.

She was a married woman at the time she went away with Sir Henry Mildmay, and this caused a trial, not for divorce, for the case was undefended, but to assess the damages, when the jury gave the large sum of £15,000, the highest damages ever given in a case of crim. con.

Lady Granville in a letter from Paris of 20 April, 1824, says, when describing people at the opera, that in one box was:—"Lady Mildmay beautiful as ever but cut in brass."

In another letter of December of the same year she writes:—"They (the French people) will scarcely look at an English man or woman out of their own peculiar set, will not admit a French one who is not à la mode, but whom does one find intimes, suivis, Et presque adorés, Lady Aldborough, Young Broadwood, and Sir Henry Mildmay." No mention of Lady Mildmay.

Lord William Lennox says of Sir Henry Mildmay that he was:—"A high bred gentleman, full of information, with only a slight tinge of puppyism."

SIR HENRY ST. JOHN CAREW ST. JOHN MILDMAY
*From coloured drawing by R. Cosway*

Lord Lamington writes in the *Days of the Dandies*:—" I will take men I have personally known, Count d'Orsay, Lord Cantelupe, Lord Chesterfield, Lord Alvanley, Sir George Womb-well, Sir Henry Mildmay, Ridley Colborne, and others. They were all men of excellent accomplishments, and dress was the least part of their merit ; they understood the value

of employing<br>Some hours to make the remnant worth enjoying.

They were always welcome guests, not only in fashionable but in grave political circles."

It seems evident, therefore, that Sir Henry was a man of very good natural abilities, and that he had improved himself intellectually. That he did not show to better advantage and establish an influential position was no doubt due to his being too well endowed with good looks and money, and to the habits, manners, and customs of the social life of his period.

Gay and interesting as was Sir Henry's life he was not always cheerful, and in a letter from 11 Belgrave Street to Miss Pigot, a constant correspondent, he writes :—

" How gloomy everything is to-day and this is merry England ! It is an atmosphere to suggest Prussic acid or a pan of charcoal, and blue devils are hopping about in every direction, and life is hardly endurable, even with a sentimental attachment, topp'd up with Roman punch. How is a

man to destroy himself decently ? I hate the idea
of hanging, drowning, razoring—besides being
vulgar and disgusting—they hurt. I have read
of people drinking themselves to death, there must
be some fun in that, so here goes, a bottle of
champagne and silence—for I have shut the
shutters

"Till Resurrection then
"Adieu dear Miss Pigot
"Yours as ever
"H. S. M."

The letter is in a collection in the Bodleian Library,
and may be called prophetic, for the last years
of Sir Henry's life were, from various reasons,
far from happy, and he ended his life by shooting
himself.

Sir Henry's son by his first wife, Henry Bouverie
Paulet St. John-Mildmay, became the fifth Baronet,
and on the death of his grandmother, Jane Lady
St. John-Mildmay, succeeded to what was left
of the family estates. The Somersetshire estate
was settled on Paulet, second son of Jane Lady
Mildmay, and the Newington property was sold
to pay the portions of her younger children.

Sir Henry, the fifth Baronet, joined the 7th
Fusiliers 8 June, 1830, exchanged to the 2nd
Dragoon Guards 7 April, 1837, and sold out
11 November, 1851, having attained the rank of
Captain and been on half-pay from 25 April, 1848.
He afterwards commanded for some time the

Hampshire Yeomanry, and retired as Honorary Colonel on the 11th March, 1882.

A picture of him at Dogmersfield by Ediss shows him in yeomanry uniform.

Sir Henry married Helena, second daughter of the Rt. Honourable Charles Shaw Lefevre, Speaker of the House of Commons, and afterwards Viscount Eversley.

When he settled at Dogmersfield he became an active magistrate of the county, was faithful to all his duties as a country gentleman, and to him may be applied the words used by Camden when writing of Sir Walter Mildmay :—"that he was one who discharged the offices of a good citizen and a good man."

He died 16 July, 1902, in his ninety-second year, and thus three successive leading representatives of the Mildmays attained to the great ages of ninety-three, ninety-two, and ninety-one.

Two of Sir Henry's half brothers, Edmond and Horace, served for a short time in the Austrian Army. Augustus, the youngest brother, died 8 March, 1839 ; Horace, the 5 May, 1866, and was buried at Milan. The eldest, Edmond, remarkable for his good looks and charm of manner, was well known in London. He was Equerry for six years to the first Duke of Cambridge, then to the late Duke of Cambridge during His Royal Highness's lifetime. He was attached to the head-quarters of the Austrian Army in Italy during the campaign of May, June, and July, 1859, receiving the

Austrian war medal. Also Secretary of the National Rifle Association from 1860 to 1890.

He was thrice married, and died 8 October, 1905, aged ninety.

Another rather well-known member of the family lately deceased, was Mr. Henry Bingham St. John-Mildmay, a partner in the old Baring house, and father of Mr. F. B. St. John-Mildmay, M.P. for the Totnes division of Devonshire. He was a man of great generosity, highly esteemed by all who knew him, and died aged seventy-seven, 1 November, 1905.

Major Henry Paulet St. John Mildmay, elder son of Sir Henry, the fifth Baronet, succeeded him as sixth Baronet. He served in the Grenadier Guards from 1872 to 1895. Became Captain 16 July, 1884 ; Major, 24 February, 1892. Was present with the Egyptian Expedition of 1882, Action of Mahuda, Battle of Tel-el-Kebir; medal and clasp, bronze star. Also in the Soudan Expedition, 1885. Mentioned in Suakim despatches 25 August, 1885. Clasp and Brevet of Major.

He was specially selected for a command in the Mounted Infantry in 1885, not only for his soldierly capacities, but also for his knowledge of and skill with horses, both of which were shown by his successes in the Household Brigade steeplechases on horses he trained and rode.

Major Sir Henry P. St. John-Mildmay's seat is at Dogmersfield Park, Winchfield, Hants, in which county he is a magistrate, a careful and considerate landlord, and a good steward of his estate.

Edmund S. P. Mildmay.

The St. John arms are 2 and 3 argent, on a chief gules, 2 mullets or. The Mildmay arms are 1 and 4 argent, 3 lions rampant, 2 and 1 azure.

The St. John motto is " Data Fata Secutus."

The Mildmay motto is " Allah Ta Hara."

The Rev. W. Betham says in his Baronetage that a Mildmay is supposed to have accompanied King Richard I to the Holy Land, and to have received for his services a motto the family bear to this day. No authority is given for the statement, nor does any seem procurable. Roger Mildmay and his brother Herbert lived in the time of Richard I, but nothing more is known of them than that their names appear in a deed of a gift of land by Herbert to Roger. Sir Walter Mildmay used the motto " Virtute non vi," and that of " Alla Ta Hara " does not appear till later, though exactly when we cannot ascertain, and it seems a pity that Sir Walter's good motto should have been discarded and a grammatically incorrect Arabic one adopted. Burke attempts the translation of " God is cleanliness, otherwise Purity," but Sir Herbert Chermside, a thorough Arabic scholar, to whom the motto was submitted, was kind enough to write to us exhaustively about it, and to express the opinion that as now written it is against the Arabic idiom, and that in transliteration the letter " s " had probably been dropped, so that the motto should really read :—

" Allah Ta Hárăs,"

which means, God has guarded.

# APPENDICES

# APPENDIX A

## GENEALOGY

(1) Hugh Mildeme.   (Probably living in 1147.)

(2) Robert Mildeme, Kt.   *m.* Matilda le Rous.

(3) Roger Mildeme of Hambledon.     Herbert. *Ob. s.p.*

(4) Roger Mildeme, Kt.   *m.* Matilda de Eltham.

(5) Henry Mildeme of Herefordshire.

(6) Ranulphe or Ralph Mildeme.

(7) Ranulphe Mildeme.

(8) Henry Mildeme of Stonhouse.

(9) Robert Mildeme.     Walter. *Ob. s.p.*

(10) Robert Mildeme.

(11) Thomas Mildeme.   *m.* Amie Kingscott.   1439.

(12) Thomas Mildeme.   *m.* Margaret Cornish, of an old Essex
family of Much Waltham.   1465.

(13) Walter Mildeme.   *m.* Margaret Everard ditto ditto 1483.

237

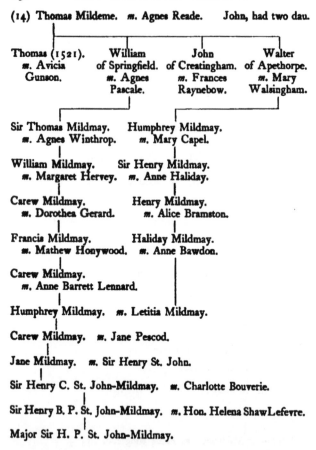

(14) Thomas Mildeme.   m. Agnes Reade.   John, had two dau.

Thomas (1521).   William   John   Walter
  m. Avicia   of Springfield.   of Creatingham.   of Apethorpe.
  Gunson.   m. Agnes   m. Frances   m. Mary
    Pascale.   Raynebow.   Walsingham.

Sir Thomas Mildmay.   Humphrey Mildmay.
  m. Agnes Winthrop.   m. Mary Capel.

William Mildmay.   Sir Henry Mildmay.
  m. Margaret Hervey.   m. Anne Haliday.

Carew Mildmay.   Henry Mildmay.
  m. Dorothea Gerard.   m. Alice Bramston.

Francis Mildmay.   Haliday Mildmay.
  m. Mathew Honywood.   m. Anne Bawdon.

Carew Mildmay.
  m. Anne Barrett Lennard.

Humphrey Mildmay.   m. Letitia Mildmay.

Carew Mildmay.   m. Jane Pescod.

Jane Mildmay.   m. Sir Henry St. John.

Sir Henry C. St. John-Mildmay.   m. Charlotte Bouverie.

Sir Henry B. P. St. John-Mildmay.   m. Hon. Helena Shaw Lefevre.

Major Sir H. P. St. John-Mildmay.

Abbreviated copies of the old documents in the possession of the Fane family giving proofs of the members of the Mildmay family in the above genealogy numbered 1 to 13, except No. 11, the letter referring to No. 11 being lost.

(1 and 2) Be it known to all men by these presents that I Count Symon on the petition of Robert Mildeme K$^t$ Son of Hugh Mildeme concede and by this charter confirm to the Church of S. Andrews of Osolvestum and the Canons there an acre of land in Twyford etc.

(2) To all men of the Mother Church present and future Matilda le Rous sends salutation. Know that I for the safety of my own soul and that of Robert Mildmey my husband give and concede to the Church of S. Andrew, Oslovesty etc.

(3) Know all men present and future that I Herbert Mildeme son of Robert Mildeme concede and by my present charter confirm to Roger my brother lands which my father gave to his son by a Charter which I have in Hous with all the lands I have in Hambledon etc.   (Sealed with one lion.)

(4) Know all men present and future that I Roger de Mildemey for the souls of my father and mother, and for the souls of my ancestors, and for the salvation of my own soul, Matilda de Eltham my wife has given to God and the blessed Mary etc.

(4) To all the Faithfull in Christ Gilbert Marshall Count of Pembroke Sends greeting, know that we concede for our own soul and the souls of our ancestors and successors etc—being a grant of money for Church Service etc—Witnessed by Walter Mar, William de la Mare, Roger filius Roger Mildeme etc.

(5 and 6) Know all men present and future that

l Henry de Mildeme son of Roger de Mildeme give and by present charter confirm to Ranulphe de Mildeme my son all my lands in Hereford which I hold of the Dominus Reginald Fitzherbert, Miles etc.

(Sealed with 3 lions rampant, 2 and 1.)

(7) Memorandum 10 Kallends of May, 7 year Edward II that Ranulph son of Ranulph de Mildeme resigns his pension of 6 marks to the Abbot and Convent of Evesham etc.

(8) Be it known to all men that I Henry de Mildeme son of Ralph de Mildeme give concede and by this charter confirm to John de Pynkenesse and John Wace, chaplains all my goods and chattels movable and immoveable in my manors of Stonhouse and Hazebear (?) at the present moment existing.

Given at Stonhouse 29 Edward III (Sealed with 3 lions).

(8) Be it known to all men that we Thomas Holland Earl of Kent and Seneschall de Wake have ordained and appointed my dear and good friend Henry Myldemay and John Wyrle Esquiers jointly and seperately my attorney to deliver seisin of all my land and tenements etc. in the town of Caleys to Thomas Strete his heirs etc. Made by me the said Thomas 16 July 15 Richard II (1392)

(9 and 10) Edmund Earl of Stafford to all whom it may concern these present writings shall cause salutations. Know that we concede and by this present charter confirm to Henry Ball in pure and

perpetual elemosynary the Church of Orwell.
Witness John de Oreby, Robert de Mildeme and
Robert his son etc. 1 April 4 Henry IV.

(10) Know all men by these presents that we
Humphrey Earl of Stafford make and ordain
Robert Mildemay, William Blower, and John
Fering my attorneys etc—2 May 17 Henry VI.

(12 and 13) This writing made the Saturday
next before the Feast of the Nativity of Our Lord
the 2 year of Henry VII witnesseth that I Thomas
Myldemey have received of John Abbot of Evesham
for my Corradie* and for the Corradie of Walter
Myldemey my son due to us from the Invention
of the Holy Cross and the Advint of S$^t$ Peter
next coming £10–0–0.

(Signed) THOMAS MYLDEMEY

(13) Know all men present and future that we
Ralph Bottesworth and William Benyt Chaplains
of Wrytell, Essex, give and concede to William
Muriell and Agnes his wife, Walter Myldemey
and Margaret his wife of Great Waltham, Co:
Essex, 12 acres of pasture lying in three crofts in
Waltham &c. S$^t$ Valentine's Day 2 Henry VII.

* Corradie, from Corradere, to scrape together or hoard.

R

# APPENDIX B

## OCCASIONAL USE OF THE NAME OF MILDMAY

A three-volume novel, entitled *Almacks*, deals largely with Mildmays. One of the principal characters being Reginald Mildmay, of a family of considerable importance and owner of Bishop's Court.

*Frank Mildmay, or the Naval Officer*, by Captain Marryat, has been previously mentioned.

There is a novel called *Louisa Mildmay, or the History of an Unfortunate*, by Kelly, wherein she from · being unfortunate becomes very fortunate. Of this heroine there are beautiful engravings, not belonging to the book, but issued separately, one being by Prattent.

Another work of fiction, called *Baby's Grandmother*, has in it a curate named Herbert Mildmay.

" Mr. Mildemay " is the Prime Minister of a Liberal Ministry in Anthony Trollope's *Phineas Finn*.

In a recent novel, entitled *My Lady Laughter*, by Mr. Dwight Tilton, dealing with the period of the siege of Boston, John Mildmay, Councillor of Boston, is introduced, and Mr. Tilton on being

242

written to affirmed that he was a real character, and not a novelist's invention. Inquiries at Boston, and an appeal to the Genealogical and Historical Society there have not elicited any information about John Mildmay.

In 1888 was published a book called *Hopelessly Irish*, by Jacob Mildmay. The publishers, Messrs. Gill and Son, of Dublin, informed us that the name was an assumed one, that the book was out of print, and that they could not recollect the real name of the writer.

In Tom Taylor's play of *Still Waters Run Deep*, the hero is John Mildmay, and a very good fellow he is.

About 1885 to 1890 an actress playing in London called herself Miss Mildmay.

In a book that has lately appeared entitled *Under the Pompadours*, by E. W. Jennings, there are several Mildmays. A Sir Henry, with vast estates near Poole, whose son and heir, Kyrle, marries the hero's sister. The villain of the book being his cousin, Chevalier Mildmay.

# APPENDIX C

## PORTRAITS OF MILDMAYS

### Dogmersfield Park

ARTIST

(1) Thomas Mildmay. Auditor of
the Court of Augmentations   Unknown

(2) Sir Thomas Mildmay of Moulsham. ½ length in armour.
Inscription "A.D. 1578 et
ætatis 38. Fortunæ O.O.
(looks older)    .    .    .     ,,

(3) Sir Walter Mildmay, Chancellor
of the Exchequer to Queen
Elizabeth. Inscription "Anno
1581. Virtute non vi"    .     ,,

(4) Sir Walter Mildmay. Panel ½
length. Inscription "Anno
1587. Ætatis 66"    .    .     ,,

(5) Sir Thomas Mildmay of Barnes.
Panel ½ length. Inscription
"1603. Æt: 62"    .    .     ,,

(6) William Mildmay, Esq., eldest
son of Sir Thomas. ¾ length     ,,

(7) Humphrey Mildmay of Danbury. Panel, small ½ length     ,,

244

ARTIST

(8) Sir Henry Mildmay. Master
of the Jewel Office. ¾ length Unknown

(9) Sir Henry Mildmay. Lying
dead on a bed covered with a
black pall, head, hands, and
feet showing. Obit circa 1664-5     „

(10) Francis Hervey Mildmay of
Marks. 1654. ½ length   .     „

(11) Charles Mildmay, Baron Fitzwalter. 1728. Bust. Oval     „

(12) Benjamin Mildmay, Earl Fitzwalter. ½ length. Oval  .     „

(13) The same. 1731. Full length     „

(14) Frances, wife of Benjamin.
1727. Full length   .    .     „

(15) Sister of Henry Mildmay of
Shawford. ¾ length. Young
girl with a dog in her arms  .     „

(16) Carew Hervey Mildmay of
Hazlegrove. 1733. ¾ length     „

(17) Edith Phelips, second wife of
Carew    .    .    .    .     „

(18) Sir William Mildmay, Bart.,
of Moulsham   .    .    .     „

(19) Anne, wife of Sir William. ¾
length   .    .    .    .     „

(20) Carew Mildmay of Shawford.
½ length   .    .    .    .     „

(21) Jane, wife of Carew. Small full
length   .    .    .    .     „

ARTIST

(22) Sir Henry St. John-Mildmay,
Bart. ½ length . . . Romney

(23)*Jane, wife of Sir Henry. Full
length with child (sold) . Hoppner

(24) Sir Henry C. St. John-Mildmay, Bart. ¾ length . . Sandars

(25) Maria and Judith Anne Mildmay. Twins. Drawing . Edridge

(26) Sir Henry B. P. St. John-Mildmay, Bart. ½ length, in
Yeomanry uniform . . Eddiss

(27) Hon. Helena, wife of Sir
Henry. ¾ length. Sitting
figure . . . . Swinton

(28) Constance and Gerald Mildmay. Large full length . Sands

In a scrapbook at Dogmersfield are several
beautifully executed Indian ink drawings, some
being of pictures whose owners are not known, as
of Sir Thomas Mildmay, 1608, Lady Frances
Radcliff, his wife, Captain Anthony Mildmay,
Humphrey Mildmay of Danbury, æt. 10, Anno
1599, from a picture in the possession of Disney
Fytche, Esq.

## Hazlegrove, Somersetshire

(1) Thomas Mildmay. Auditor . Janssen (?)

(2) Humphrey Mildmay of Marks
and Shawford. On copper . Unknown

(3) Sir William Mildmay . . ,,

* There are fine Mezzotints by Joy of this picture.

ARTIST

(4) Carew Hervey Mildmay.  Red
    cap of Bachelor of Music  . Thornhill
(5) Same.  Full length     .    . Vandermeyen
(6) Carew Hervey Mildmay.  Full
    length   .   .   .   .    ,,
(7) Edith, second wife of Carew  . Shackleton
(8) Jane, Lady St. John-Mildmay.
    Drawing   .   .   .   . Harlow
(9) Paulet St. John-Mildmay    . Saunders
(10) Mrs. Paulet     .    .    .    ,,
(11) Paulet St. John-Mildmay.  Col-
    oured Drawing  .   .   . Edridge
(12) Paulet St. John-Mildmay, Junr.
    Uncoloured Drawing  .   .   ,,
(13) Arundel and Meriel St. John-
    Mildmay  .   .   .   . Unknown

### 46 Berkeley Square

(1) Humphrey Mildmay, second son
    of  Carew  Hervey  Mildmay
    of  Marks  and  Anne  Barrett
    Lennard.  ½ length   .    . Unknown
(2) Carew  Hervey  Mildmay  of
    Hazlegrove.  ½ length .   .    ,,

### 28 Portman Square

(1) Miss Beatrice St. John-Mildmay  Wm. Logsdail

### Edge Grove, Watford

(1) Jane, Lady St. John-Mildmay.
    ¾ length   .   .   .   . Downman

ARTIST

(2) Frances Lucy Penelope Perceval,
second wife of Capt. Edward
St. John-Mildmay. Very fine
full-length picture of a girl . Unknown

(3) Miss Warde, wife of Walter
St. John-Mildmay, Esqre.
Beautiful drawing, head and
bust coloured . . . „

### 12 Upper Brook Street

(1) Judith Anne, Countess of
Radnor. ¾ length. There
are small replicas of this
picture that belonged to Mrs.
Ellis and Lady Penzance . Saunders

### Corsham Court

(1) Jane, Lady St. John-Mildmay . Downman

### Foulis Court, Eastleigh

(1) Letitia Mildmay, wife of George
Ricketts, Esq., of Lainstone
Sir Wm. Beechey

### Colonel George Maxwell

(1) Anne Mildmay, wife of George
Clerk, Esq. Drawing . . Unknown

### Mereworth Castle

(1) Mary Mildmay, wife of Sir
Francis Fane. Full length
with child . . . . „

## 31 Gloucester Street, S.W.

ARTIST

(1) Sir Henry P. St. John-Mildmay,
   Bart. Miniature  .    .    . Unknown

(2) Jane, wife of Sir Henry. Miniature  .    .    .    .    .    "

(3) Mrs. George Wm. St. John-
   Mildmay  .    .    .    . Ollivier

(4) Mrs. George Wm. St. John-
   Mildmay. Oval .    .    . A. Lumley

(5) Lt.-Col. Herbert St. John-Mildmay, as a boy in kilt. Water-
   colour    .    .    .    . Unknown

(6) Lt.-Col. Herbert St. John-Mildmay, working at a carpenter's
   bench  .    .    .    . Barnard

(7) Mrs. Herbert St. John-Mildmay. Oval water-colour    . Unknown

(8) Mrs. Herbert St. John-Mildmay. Pastel    .    .    . Miss Purser

## Knole Park

(1) Sir Walter Mildmay. ½ length.
   Panel     .    .    .    . Unknown

## Fulbeck

(1) Sir Walter Mildmay. ¾ length.
   Panel    .    .    .    "

(2) Sir Anthony Mildmay. Full
   length  .    .    .    .    "

(3) Grace, wife of Sir Anthony. Full
   length  .    .    .    .    "

(4) Mary, daughter of Sir Anthony Mytens

### Hever Castle, Kent

ARTIST

(1) Paulet St. John-Mildmay, as a boy. Full length. (Bought for £10,500) . . . Hoppner

### The late Edgar Disney, Esq.

(1) Cecilia Mildmay of Danbury . Unknown

### Emmanuel College, Cambridge

(1) Sir Walter Mildmay. ¾ length. Panel. Inscription "A.D. 1574. Ætatis 53. Virtute non vi. Sir Walter Mildmay" . . Unknown

(2) Sir Walter Mildmay. ¾ length. Panel. Inscription "Virtute non vi. A° Dom. 1579" . „

(3) Sir Walter Mildmay, ½ length. Inscriptions on two scrolls "Vera effigies Walter Mildmay equitis," "Collegii Emmanuelis Cantabrigii Fundator" „

(4) Sir Walter Mildmay. ½ length. „

(5) „ „ „ „

(6) „ „ Full length. Inscription "An: Dom: 1588. Ætat suæ 66. Virtute non vi." Van Somer

(7) Mary, wife to Sir Walter. ¾ length. Panel. Inscription "A.D. 1574. ÆTATIS SUÆ 46. Lady Mildmay wife to Sir Walter" . . . . Unknown

(8) Sir Anthony Mildmay. Full
length . . . . Unknown<sup>ARTIST</sup>

### Watts Gallery, near Guildford

(1) Miss Mildmay. (? which Miss
Mildmay) . . . . Watts

In the printed list of Downman
portraits are the following

(1) Jane, Lady Mildmay. ½ length.
1793.
(2) Jane, Lady Mildmay. ½ length.
1793.
(3) Mrs. George Ricketts (Letitia
Mildmay). ½ length. 1793.
(4) Mrs. George Ricketts (Letitia
Mildmay). ½ length. 1793.

There are, besides, several lithographs and
prints of Mildmays, such as Sir H. P. St. John-
Mildmay, Capt. George Wm. St. John-Mildmay,
Capt. Edmond St. John-Mildmay, Mr. Horace
St. John-Mildmay, etc., mostly from drawings by
Count d'Orsay.

# APPENDIX D

## Lord Lieutenant, Essex

1730. Benjamin Mildmay, Earl Fitzwalter

## Sheriffs, Essex

1558. Thomas Mildmay of Chelmsford.
1572. Sir Thomas Mildmay of Moulsham.
1593. Humphrey Mildmay of Danbury.
1597. Thomas Mildmay of Springfield Barnes.
1609. Sir Thomas Mildmay of Moulsham.
1629. Sir Henry Mildmay of Woodham Walters.
1636. Sir Humphrey Mildmay of Danbury.
1712. Carew Hervey Mildmay of Marks.
1765. Sir William Mildmay of Moulsham

## Hampshire

1668. Henry Mildmay of Shawford.
1787. Sir Henry P. St. John-Mildmay of
Dogmersfield.
1862. Sir Henry B. P. St. John-Mildmay
Dogmersfield.

## Hertfordshire

1606. Sir Walter Mildmay of Pishiobury.

# APPENDIX E

## SOME MARRIAGES NOT MENTIONED IN THE MEMOIR

1548. October 10. Edward Mylmaye and Joanna Auparte.

1583. September 6. John Mildmay and Margaret Knight.

1586. November 23. Andrew Attwood and Marion Mildmay, daughter of John Mildmay of Creatingham, deceased.

1597. August 27. George Burghley, rector of Laurence Dengey, Essex, and Emma, widow of John Mildmay, late of Prittlewell, and eldest son of John Mildmay of Creatingham.

1613. August 16. Thomas Mildmay and Margaret Harberd.

1617–8. January 2. W. Nutbrowne of Hornchurch, Essex, and Frances Mildmay, daughter of William Mildmay, deceased.

1621. July 9. Walter Mildmay and Mary Bond.

1630. May 10. R. Harlakenden of Earl's Cone, Essex, and Alice, daughter of Sir Henry Mildmay of Graces.

1637. May 20. H. Bigge of Cressing Temple, Essex, and Anne Mildmay of Tarling, by consent of her uncle Robert Mildmay of Tarling.

1662. December 19. Humphrey Mildmay of Danbury and Catherine Steele.

1668-9. January 4. John Mildmay, merchant, London, and Mary Chamberlaine.

1669-70. February 15. Robert Mildmay of Gray's Inn and Mary Rosseter.

1672. April 22. William Mildmay of St. Giles' in the Fields and Frances Carr.

1672. November 25. William Chapman of St. Martin's in the Fields and Amy Mildmay of Tarling.

1674. October 22. Mathew Lister and Frances Mildmay of Heston, Middlesex.

1675. July 7. Vincent Amcotes of Amcotes, Co. Lincoln, and Amey Mildmay of Graces.

1676. February 14. Timothy Whitfeild of Gray's Inn and Mary Mildmay of St. Bride's.

1678. December 5. William Mildmay of Lambeth, widower, and Elizabeth Chislett.

1678. December 6. Sir Drayner Massingberd of South Ormsby, Lincoln, and Anne Mildmay of Harrington, same county.

1686. June 30. Thomas Gardner and Lucy Mildmay of Graces.

1689. October 22. Christopher Fowler and Frances Mildmay of Graces.

1691. December 11. Charles Goodwin of Great Baddow and Mary Mildmay of Graces.

1696. September 7. Edmund Waterson and Elizabeth Mildmay of Graces.

1698. April 19. Lawrence St. Lo of St. James's, Westminster, and Ann Mildmay.

1706. December 16. John Searle, D.D., Rector of Willingale Doe, Essex, and Judith Mildmay of Hornchurch, same county.

# LIVING MASTERS OF MUSIC.

An Illustrated Series of Monographs dealing with Contemporary Musical Life, and including Representatives of all Branches of the Art.

### Edited by ROSA NEWMARCH.

Crown 8vo.    Cloth.    Price 2/6 net.

HENRY J. WOOD.  By ROSA NEWMARCH.
SIR EDWARD ELGAR.  By R. J. BUCKLEY.
JOSEPH JOACHIM.  By J. A. FULLER MAITLAND.
EDWARD A. MACDOWELL.  By LAWRENCE GILMAN.
THEODOR LESCHETIZKY.  By ANNETTE HULLAH.
GIACOMO PUCCINI.  By WAKELING DRY.
IGNAZ PADEREWSKI.  By E. A. BAUGHAN.
CLAUDE DEBUSSY.  By MRS. FRANZ LIEBICH.
RICHARD STRAUSS.  By ERNEST NEWMAN.

# STARS OF THE STAGE

A SERIES OF ILLUSTRATED BIOGRAPHIES OF THE LEADING ACTORS, ACTRESSES, AND DRAMATISTS.

### Edited by J. T. GREIN.

Crown 8vo.  Price 2/6 each net.

ELLEN TERRY.  By CHRISTOPHER ST. JOHN.
SIR HERBERT BEERBOHM TREE.  By MRS. GEORGE CRAN.
SIR W. S. GILBERT.  By EDITH A. BROWNE.
SIR CHARLES WYNDHAM.  By FLORENCE TEIGNMOUTH SHORE.

# A CATALOGUE OF
## MEMOIRS, BIOGRAPHIES, ETC.

**THE LAND OF TECK & ITS SURROUNDINGS.**
By Rev. S. BARING-GOULD. With numerous Illustrations (including several in Colour) reproduced from unique originals. Demy 8vo. (9 × 5¾ inches.) 10s. 6d. net.

**AN IRISH BEAUTY OF THE REGENCY : By**
MRS. WARRENNE BLAKE. Author of "Memoirs of a Vanished Generation, 1813-1855." With a Photogravure Frontispiece and other Illustrations. Demy 8vo. (9 × 5¾ inches.) 16s. net.

\*\* The Irish Beauty is the Hon. Mrs. Calvert, daughter of Viscount Pery, Speaker of the Irish House of Commons, and wife of Nicholson Calvert, M. P., of Hunsdon. Born in 1767, Mrs. Calvert lived to the age of ninety-two, and there are many people still living who remember her. In the delightful journals, now for the first time published, exciting events are described.

**NAPOLEON IN CARICATURE : 1795-1821. By**
A. M. BROADLEY. With an Introductory Essay on Pictorial Satire as a Factor in Napoleonic History, by J. HOLLAND ROSE, Litt. D. (Cantab.). With 24 full-page Illustrations in Colour and upwards of 200 in Black and White from rare and unique originals. 2 Vols. Demy 8vo. (9 × 5¾ inches.) 42s. net.

*Also an Edition de Luxe.* 10 guineas net.

**MEMORIES OF SIXTY YEARS AT ETON,**
CAMBRIDGE AND ELSEWHERE. By ROBERT BROWNING. Illustrated. Demy 8vo. (9 × 5¾ inches.) 14s. net.

**THE FOUNDATIONS OF THE NINETEENTH**
CENTURY. By STEWART HOUSTON CHAMBERLAIN. A Translation from the German by JOHN LEES. With an Introduction by LORD REDESDALE. Demy 8vo. (9 × 5¾ inches.) 2 vols. 25s. net.

**THE SPEAKERS OF THE HOUSE OF**
COMMONS from the Earliest Times to the Present Day, with a Topographical Account of Westminster at various Epochs, Brief Notes on sittings of Parliament and a Retrospect of the principal Constitutional Changes during Seven Centuries. By ARTHUR IRWIN DASENT, Author of "The Life and Letters of JOHN DELANE," "The History of St. James's Square," etc. etc. With numerous Portraits, including two in Photogravure and one in Colour. Demy 8vo. (9 × 5¾ inches.) 21s. net.

## WILLIAM HARRISON AINSWORTH AND

HIS FRIENDS. By S. M. ELLIS. With upwards of 50 Illustrations, 4 in Photogravure. 2 vols. Demy 8vo. (9 × 5¾ inches.) 32s. net.

## NAPOLEON AND KING MURAT. 1808-1815:

A Biography compiled from hitherto Unknown and Unpublished Documents. By ALBERT ESPITALIER. Translated from the French by J. LEWIS MAY. With a Photogravure Frontispiece and 16 other Illustrations. Demy 8vo. (9 × 5¾ inches.) 12s. 6d. net.

## LADY CHARLOTTE SCHREIBER'S JOURNALS

Confidences of a Collector of Ceramics and Antiques throughout ¹⁻ Britain, France, Germany, Italy, Spain, Holland, Belgium, Switzerland, and Turkey. From the Year 1869 to 1885. Edited MONTAGUE GUEST, with Annotations by EGAN MEW. With upwards of 100 Illustrations, including 8 in colour and 2 in photogravure. Royal 8vo. 2 Volumes. 42s. net.

## CHARLES DE BOURBON, CONSTABLE OF

FRANCE: "THE GREAT CONDOTTIERE." By CHRISTOPHER HARE. With a Photogravure Frontispiece and 16 other Illustrations. Demy 8vo. (9 × 5¾ inches.) 12s. 6d. net.

## THE NELSONS OF BURNHAM THORPE: A

Record of a Norfolk Family compiled from Unpublished Letters and Note Books, 1787-1843. Edited by M. EYRE MATCHAM. With a Photogravure Frontispiece and 16 other Illustrations. Demy 8vo. (9 × 5¾ inches.) 16s. net.

*₊* This interesting contribution to Nelson literature is drawn from the journals and correspondence of the Rev. Edmund Nelson. Rector of Burnham Thorpe and his youngest daughter, the father and sister of Lord Nelson. The Rector was evidently a man of broad views and sympathies, for we find him maintaining friendly relations with his son and daughter-in-law after their separation. What is even more strange, he felt perfectly at liberty to go direct from the house of Mrs. Horatio Nelson in Norfolk to that of Sir. William and Lady Hamilton in London, where his son was staying. This book shows how completely and without reserve the family received Lady Hamilton.

## A QUEEN OF SHREDS AND PATCHES: The

Life of Madame Tallien Notre Dame de Thermidor. From the last days of the French Revolution, until her death as Princess Chimay in 1835. By L. GASTINE. Translated from the French by J. LEWIS MAY. With a Photogravure Frontispiece and 16 other Illustrations. Demy 8vo. (9 × 5¾ inches.) 12s. 6d. net.

## SOPHIE DAWES, QUEEN OF CHANTILLY.

By VIOLETTE M. MONTAGU. Author of "The Scottish College in Paris," etc. With a Photogravure Frontispiece and 16 other Illustrations and Three Plans. Demy 8vo. (9 × 5¾ inches.) 12s. 6d. net.

\*\*\*Among the many queens of France, queens by right of marriage with the reigning sovereign, queens of beauty or of intrigue, the name of Sophie Dawes, the daughter of humble fisherfolk in the Isle of Wight, better known as "the notorious Mme. de Feucheres," "The Queen of Chantilly" and "The Montespan de Saint Leu" in the land which she chose as a suitable sphere in which to excercise her talents for money-making and for getting on in the world, stand forth as a proof of what a women's will can accomplish when that will is accompanied with an uncommon share of intelligence.

## MARGARET OF FRANCE DUCHESS OF

SAVOY. 1523-1574. A Biography with Photogravure Frontispiece and 16 other Illustrations and Facsimile Reproductions of Hitherto Unpublished Letters. Demy 8vo. (9 × 5¾ inches.) 12s. 6d. net.

\*\*\*A time when the Italians are celebrating the Jubliee of the Italian Kingdom is perhaps no unfitting moment in which to glance back over the annals of that royal House of Savoy which has rendered Italian unity possible. Margaret of France may without exaggeration be counted among the builders of modern Italy. She married Emanuel Philibert, the founder of Savoyard greatness: and from the day of her marriage until the day of her death she laboured to advance the interests of her adopted land.

## MADAME DE BRINVILLIERS AND HER

TIMES. 1630-1676. By HUGH STOKES. With a Photogravure Frontispiece and 16 other Illustrations. Demy 8vo. (9 × 5¾ inches.) 12s. 6d. net.

\*\*\* The name of Marie Marguerite d'Aubray, Marquise de Brinvilliers, is famous is famous in the annals of crime, but the true history of her career is little known. A woman of birth and rank, she was also a remorseless poisoner, and her trial was one of the most sensational episodes of the early reign of Louis XIV. The author was attracted to this curious subject by Charles le Brun's realistic sketch of the unhappy Marquise as she appeared on her way to execution. This *chief d'oeuvre* of misery and agony forms the frontispiece to the volume, and strikes a fitting keynote to an absorbing story of human passion and wrong-doing.

## THE VICISSITUDES OF A LADY-IN-WAITING.

1735-1821. By EUGENE WELVERT. Translated from the French by LILIAN O'NEILL. With a Photogravure Frontispiece and 16 other Illustrations. Demy 8vo. (9 × 5¾ inches.) 12s. 6d. net.

\*\*\* The Duchesse de Narbonne-Lara was Lady-in-Waiting to Madame Adelaide, the eldest daughter of Louis XV. Around the stately figure of this Princess are gathered the most remarkable characters of the days of the Old Regime, the Revolution and the fist Empire. The great charm of the work is that it takes us over so much and varied ground. Here, in the gay crowd of ladies and courtiers, in the rustle of flowery silken paniers, in the clatter of high-heeled shoes, move the figures of Louis XV., Louis XVI., Du Barri and Marie-Antoinette. We catch picturesque glimpses of the great wits, diplomatists and soldiers of the time, until, finally we encounter Napoléon Bonaparte.

**ANNALS OF A YORKSHIRE HOUSE.** From the Papers of a Macaroni and his Kindred. By A. M.W. STIRLING, author of "Coke of Norfolk and his Friends." With 33 Illustrations, including 3 in Colour and 3 in Photogravure. Demy 8vo. (9 × 5¾ inches.) 2 vols. 32s. net.

**MINIATURES :** A Series of Reproductions in Photogravure of Eighty-Five Miniatures of Distinguished Personages, including Queen Alexandra, the Queen of Norway, the Princess Royal, and the Princess Victoria. Painted by CHARLES TURRELL. (Folio.) The Edition is limited to One Hundred Copies for sale in England and America, and Twenty-Five Copies for Presentation, Review, and the Museums. Each will be Numbered and Signed by the Artist. 15 guineas net.

**THE LAST JOURNALS OF HORACE** WALPOLE. During the Reign of George III. from 1771-1783. With Notes by Dr. DORAN. Edited with an Introduction by A. FRANCIS STEUART, and containing numerous Portraits reproduced from contemporary Pictures, Engravings, etc. 2 vols. Demy 8vo. (9 × 5¾ inches.) 25s. net.

**THE WAR IN WEXFORD.** By H. F. B. WHEELER AND A. M. BROADLEY. An Account of The Rebellion in South of Ireland in 1798, told from Original Documents. With numerous Reproductions of contemporary Portraits and Engravings. Demy 8vo. (9 × 5¾ inches.) 12s. 6d. net.

**RECOLLECTIONS OF GUY DE MAUPASSANT.** by His Valet FRANÇOIS. Translated from the French by MAURICE REYNOLD. Demy 8vo. (9 × 5¾ inches.) 7s. 6d. net.

**FAMOUS AMERICANS IN PARIS.** By JOHN JOSEPH CONWAY, M.A. With 32 Full-page Illustrations. Demy 8vo. (9 × 5¾ inches.) 10s. 6d. net.

**LIFE AND MEMOIRS OF JOHN CHURTON** COLLINS. Written and Compiled by his son, L. C. COLLINS. Demy 8vo. (9 × 5¾ inches.) 7s. 6d. net.

### THE WIFE OF GENERAL BONAPARTE. By

Joseph Turquan. Author of "The Love Affairs of Napoleon," etc. Translated from the French by Miss Violette Montagu. With a Photogravure Frontispiece and 16 other Illustrations. Demy 8vo. (9 × 5¾ inches.) 12s. 6d. net.

*⁎* Although much has been written concerning the Empress Josephine, we know comparatively little about the *veuve* Beauharnais and the *citoyenne* Bonaparte, whose inconsiderate conduct during her husband's absence caused him so much anguish. We are so accustomed to consider Josephine as the innocent victim of a cold and calculating tyrant who allowed nothing, neither human lives nor natural affections, to stand in the way of his all-conquering will, that this volume will come to us rather as a surprise. Modern historians are over-fond of blaming Napoleon for having divorced the companion of his early years; but after having read the above work, the reader will be constrained to admire General Bonaparte's forbearance and will wonder how he ever came to allow her to play the Queen at the Tuileries.

### A SISTER OF PRINCE RUPERT. ELIZABETH

PRINCESS PALATINE, ABBESS OF HERFORD. By Elizabeth Godfrey. With numerous Illustrations. Demy 8vo. (9 × 5¾ inches.) 12s. 6d. net.

### AUGUSTUS SAINT GAUDENS : an Appreciation.

By C. Lewis Hind. Illustrated with 47 full-page Reproductions from his most famous works. With a portrait of Keynon Cox. Large 4to. 12s. 6d. net.

### JOHN LOTHROP MOTLEY AND HIS FAMILY:

By Mrs. Herbert St. John Mildmay. Further Letters and Records, edited by his Daughter and Herbert St. John Mildmay, with numerous Illustrations. Demy 8vo. (9 × 5¾ inches.) 16s. net.

### SIMON BOLIVAR : El Libertador. A Life of the

Leader of the Venezuelan Revolt against Spain. By F. Loraine Petre. With a Map and Illustrations. Demy 8vo. (9 × 5¾ inches.) 12s. 6d. net.

### A LIFE OF SIR JOSEPH BANKS, PRESIDENT

OF THE ROYAL SOCIETY : With Some Notices of His Friends and Contemporaries. By Edward Smith, F.R.H.S., Author of "William Cobbett : a Biography," England and America after the Independence," etc. With a Portrait in Photogravure and 16 other Illustration. Demy 8 vo. (9 × 5¾ inches.) 12s. 6d. net.

*⁎* "The greatest living Englishman" was the tribute of his Continental contemporaries to Sir. Joseph Banks. The author of his "Life" has, with some enthusiasm, sketched the record of a man who for a period of half a century filled a very prominent place in society, but whose name is almost forgotten by the present generation.

## NAPOLEON & THE INVASION OF ENGLAND :

The Story of the Great Terror, 1797-1805. By H. F. B. WHEELER and A. M. BROADLEY. With upwards of 100 Full-page Illustrations reproduced from Contemporary Portraits, Prints, etc. ; eight in Colour. 2 Volumes. Demy 8vo. (9 × 5¾ inches.) 32s. net.

*Outlook.*—'The book is not merely one to be ordered from the library ; it should be purchased, kept on an accessible shelf, and constantly studied by all Englishmen who love England."

## DUMOURIEZ AND THE DEFENCE OF

ENGLAND AGAINST NAPOLEON. By J. HOLLAND ROSE, Litt.D. (Cantab.), Author of "The Life of Napoleon," and A. M. BROADLEY, joint-author of "Napoleon and the Invasion of England." Illustrated with numerous Portraits, Maps, and Facsimiles. Demy 8vo. (9 × 5¾ inches.) 21s. net.

## THE FALL OF NAPOLEON. By OSCAR

BROWNING, M.A., Author of "The Boyhood and Youth of Napoleon." With numerous Full-page Illustrations. Demy 8vo (9 × 5¾ inches). 12s. 6d. net.

*Spectator.*—"Without doubt Mr. Oscar Browning has produced a book which should have its place in any library of Napoleonic literature."

*Truth.*—"Mr. Oscar Browning has made not the least, but the most of the romantic material at his command for the story of the fall of the greatest figure in history."

## THE BOYHOOD & YOUTH OF NAPOLEON,

1769-1793. Some Chapters on the early life of Bonaparte. By OSCAR BROWNING. M.A. With numerous Illustrations, Portraits etc. Crown 8vo. 5s. net.

*Daily News.*—"Mr. Browning has with patience, labour, careful study, and excellent taste given us a very valuable work, which will add materially to the literature on this most fascinating of human personalities.

## THE LOVE AFFAIRS OF NAPOLEON. By

JOSEPH TURQUAN. Translated from the French by JAMES L. MAY. With 32 Full-page Illustrations. Demy 8vo. (9 × 5¾ inches). 12s. 6d. net.

## THE DUKE OF REICHSTADT(NAPOLEON II.)

By EDWARD DE WERTHEIMER. Translated from the German. With numerous Illustrations. Demy 8vo. (9 × 5¾ inches.) 21s. net. (Second Edition.)

*Times.*—"A most careful and interesting work which presents the first complete and authoritative account of this unfortunate Prince."

*Westminster Gazette.*—"This book, admirably produced, reinforced by many additional portraits, is a solid contribution to history and a monument of patient, well-applied research."

## NAPOLEON'S CONQUEST OF PRUSSIA, 1806.

By F. LORAINE PETRE. With an Introduction by FIELD-MARSHAL EARL ROBERTS, V.C., K.G., etc. With Maps, Battle Plans, Portraits, and 16 Full-page Illustrations. Demy 8vo. (9 × 5¾ inches). 12s. 6d. net.

*Scotsman.*—"Neither too concise, nor too diffuse, the book is eminently readable. It is the best work in English on a somewhat circumscribed subject."

*Outlook.*—"Mr. Petre has visited the battlefields and read everthing, and his monograph is a model of what military history, handled with enthusiasm and literary ability, can be."

## NAPOLEON'S CAMPAIGN IN POLAND, 1806-1807.

A Military History of Napoleon's First War with Russia, verified from unpublished official documents. By F. LORAINE PETRE. With 16 Full-page Illustrations, Maps, and Plans. New Edition. Demy 8vo. (9 × 5¾ inches). 12s. 6d. net.

*Army and Navy Chronicle.*—"We welcome a second edition of this valuable work. . . . Mr. Loraine Petre is an authority on the wars of the great Napoleon, and has brought the greatest care and energy into his studies of the subject."

## NAPOLEON AND THE ARCHDUKE CHARLES.

A History of the Franco-Austrian Campaign in the Valley of the Danube in 1809. By F. LORAINE PETRE. With 8 Illustrations and 6 sheets of Maps and Plans. Demy 8vo. (9 × 5¾ inches). 12s. 6d. net.

## RALPH HEATHCOTE. Letters of a Diplomatist

During the Time of Napoleon, Giving an Account of the Dispute between the Emperor and the Elector of Hesse. By COUNTESS GUNTHER GRÖBEN. With Numerous Illustrations. Demy 8vo. (9 × 5¾ inches). 12s. 6d. net.

## MEMOIRS OF THE COUNT DE CARTRIE.

A record of the extraordinary events in the life of a French Royalist during the war in La Vendée, and of his flight to Southampton, where he followed the humble occupation of gardener. With an introduction by FRÉDÉRIC MASSON, Appendices and Notes by PIERRE AMÉDÉE PICHOT, and other hands, and numerous Illustrations, including a Photogravure Portrait of the Author. Demy 8vo. (9 × 5¾ inches.) 12s. 6d. net.

*Daily News.*—"We have seldom met with a human document which has interested us so much."

## THE JOURNAL OF JOHN MAYNE DURING
A TOUR ON THE CONTINENT UPON ITS RE-
OPENING AFTER THE FALL OF NAPOLEON, 1814.
Edited by his Grandson, JOHN MAYNE COLLES. With 16
Illustrations. Demy 8vo (9 × 5¾ inches). 12s. 6d. net.

## WOMEN OF THE SECOND EMPIRE.
Chronicles of the Court of Napoleon III. By FRÉDÉRIC LOLIÉE.
With an introduction by RICHARD WHITEING, and 53 full-page
Illustrations, 3 in Photogravure. Demy 8vo. (9 × 5¾ inches.)
21s. net.

*Standard.*—"M. Frederic Loliee has written a remarkable book, vivid and pitiless in
its description of the intrigue and dare-devil spirit which flourished unchecked at
the French Court. . . . Mr. Richard Whiteing's introduction is written with
restraint and dignity.

## MEMOIRS OF MADEMOISELLE DES
ECHEROLLES. Translated from the French by MARIE
CLOTHILDE BALFOUR. With an introduction by G. K. FORTESCUE,
Portraits, etc. 5s. net.

*Liverpool Mercury.*—". . . this absorbing book. . . . The work has a very
decided historical value. The translation is excellent, and quite notable in the
preservation of idiom.

## GIOVANNI BOCCACCIO: A BIOGRAPHICAL
STUDY. By EDWARD HUTTON. With a Photogravure Frontispiece and numerous other Illustrations. Demy 8vo. (9 × 5¾
inches) 16s. net.

## THE LIFE OF PETER ILICH TCHAIKOVSKY
(1840-1893). By his Brother, MODESTE TCHAIKOVSKY. Edited
and abridged from the Russian and German Editions by ROSA
NEWMARCH. With Numerous Illustrations and Facsimiles and an
Introduction by the Editor. Demy 8vo. (9 × 5¾ inches.)
7s. 6d. net. Second edition.

*The Times.*—"A most illuminating commentary on Tchaikovsky's music."

*World.*—"One of the most fascinating self-revelations by an artist which has been
given to the world. The translation is excellent, and worth reading for its own
sake."

*Contemporary Review.*—"The book's appeal is, of course, primarily to the music-lover ;
but there is so much of human and literary interest in it, such intimate revelation
of a singularly interesting personality, that many who have never come under the
spell of the Pathetic Symphony will be strongly attracted by what is virtually the
spiritual autobiography of its composer. High praise is due to the translator and
editor for the literary skill with which she has prepared the English version of
this fascinating work. . . There have been few collections of letters published
within recent years that give so vivid a portrait of the writer as that presented to
us in these pages."

## THE LIFE OF SIR HALLIDAY MACART-
NEY, K.C.M.G., Commander of Li Hung Chang's trained
force in the Taeping Rebellion, founder of the first Chinese
Arsenal, Secretary to the first Chinese Embassy to Europe.
Secretary and Councillor to the Chinese Legation in London for
thirty years. By DEMETRIUS C. BOULGER, Author of the
"History of China," the "Life of Gordon," etc. With Illus-
trations. Demy 8vo. (9 × 5¾ inches.) Price 21s. net.

## DEVONSHIRE CHARACTERS AND STRANGE
EVENTS. By S. BARING-GOULD, M.A., Author of "Yorkshire
Oddities," etc. With 58 Illustrations. Demy 8vo. (9 × 5¾
inches.) 21s. net.

*Daily News.*—"A fascinating series . . . the whole book is rich in human interest.
It is by personal touches, drawn from traditions and memories, that the dead men
surrounded by the curious panoply of their time, are made to live again in Mr.
Baring-Gould's pages."

## THE HEART OF GAMBETTA. Translated
from the French of FRANCIS LAUR by VIOLETTE MONTAGU.
With an Introduction by JOHN MACDONALD, Portraits and other
Illustrations. Demy 8vo. (9 × 5¾ inches.) 7s. 6d. net.

*Daily Telegraph.*—"It is Gambetta pouring out his soul to Léonie Leon, the strange,
passionate, masterful demagogue, who wielded the most persuasive oratory of
modern times, acknowledging his idol, his inspiration, his Egeria."

## THE LIFE OF JOAN OF ARC. By ANATOLE
FRANCE. A Translation by WINIFRED STEPHENS. With 8 Illustrations. Demy 8vo (9 × 5¾ inches). 2 vols. Price 25s. net.

## THE DAUGHTER OF LOUIS XVI. Marie-
Thérèse-Charlotte of France, Duchesse D'Angoulême. By G.
LENOTRE. With 13 Full-page Illustrations. Demy 8vo. (9 × 5¾
inches.) Price 10s. 6d. net.

## WITS, BEAUX, AND BEAUTIES OF THE
GEORGIAN ERA. By JOHN FYVIE, author of "Some Famous
Women of Wit and Beauty," "Comedy Queens of the Georgian
Era," etc. With a Photogravure Portrait and numerous other
Illustrations. Demy 8vo (9 × 5¾ inches). 12s. 6d. net.

## MADAME DE MAINTENON : Her Life and
Times, 1655-1719. By C. C. DYSON. With 1 Photogravure
Plate and 16 other Illustrations. Demy 8vo. (9 × 5¾ inches).
12s. 6d. net.

## DR. JOHNSON AND MRS. THRALE. By

A. M. BROADLEY. With an Introductory Chapter by THOMAS SECCOMBE. With 24 Illustrations from rare originals, including a reproduction in colours of the Fellowes Miniature of Mrs. Piozzi by Roche, and a Photogravure of Harding's sepia drawing of Dr. Johnson. Demy 8vo (9 × 5¾ inches). 16s. net.

## THE DAYS OF THE DIRECTOIRE. By

ALFRED ALLINSON, M.A. With 48 Full-page Illustrations, including many illustrating the dress of the time. Demy 8vo (9 × 5¾ inches). 16s. net.

## HUBERT AND JOHN VAN EYCK : Their Life

and Work. By W. H. JAMES WEALE. With 41 Photogravure and 95 Black and White Reproductions. Royal 4to. £5 5s. net.

SIR MARTIN CONWAY'S NOTE.

Nearly half a century has passed since Mr. W. H. James Weale, then resident at Bruges, began that long series of patient investigations into the history of Netherlandish art which was destined to earn so rich a harvest. When he began work Memlinc was still called Hemling, and was fabled to have arrived at Bruges as a wounded soldier. The van Eycks were little more than legendary heroes. Roger Van der Weyden was little more than a name. Most of the other great Netherlandish artists were either wholly forgotten or named only in connection with paintings with which they had nothing to do. Mr. Weale discovered Gerard David, and disentangled his principal works from Memlinc's, with which they were then confused.

## VINCENZO FOPPA OF BRESCIA, FOUNDER OF

THE LOMBARD SCHOOL, HIS LIFE AND WORK. By CONSTANCE JOCELYN FFOULKES and MONSIGNOR RODOLFO MAJOCCHI, D.D., Rector of the Collegio Borromeo, Pavia. Based on research in the Archives of Milan, Pavia, Brescia, and Genoa and on the study of all his known works. With over 100 Illustrations, many in Photogravure, and 100 Documents. Royal 4to. £5 5s. 0d. net.

## MEMOIRS OF THE DUKES OF URBINO.

Illustrating the Arms, Art and Literature of Italy from 1440 to 1630. By JAMES DENNISTOUN of Dennistoun. A New Edition edited by EDWARD HUTTON, with upwards of 100 Illustrations. Demy 8vo. (9 × 5¾ inches.) 3 vols. 42s. net.

## THE DIARY OF A LADY-IN-WAITING. By

LADY CHARLOTTE BURY. Being the Diary Illustrative of the Times of George the Fourth. Interspersed with original Letters from the late Queen Caroline and from various other distinguished persons New edition. Edited, with an Introduction, by A. FRANCIS STEUART. With numerous portraits. Two Vols. Demy 8vo. (9 × 5¾ inches.) 21s. net.

**THE LAST JOURNALS OF HORACE WAL-POLE.** During the Reign of George III from 1771 to 1783. With Notes by Dr. Doran. Edited with an Introduction by A. Francis Steuart, and containing numerous Portraits (2 in Photogravure) reproduced from contemporary Pictures, Engravings, etc. 2 vols. Uniform with "The Diary of a Lady-in-Waiting." Demy 8vo. (9 × 5¾ inches). 25s. net.

**JUNIPER HALL :** Rendezvous of certain illustrious Personages during the French Revolution, including Alexander D'Arblay and Fanny Burney. Compiled by Constance Hill. With numerous Illustrations by Ellen G. Hill, and reproductions from various Contemporary Portraits. Crown 8vo. 5s. net.

**JANE AUSTEN :** Her Homes and Her Friends. By Constance Hill. Numerous Illustrations by Ellen G. Hill, together with Reproductions from Old Portraits, etc. Cr. 8vo 5s. net.

**THE HOUSE IN ST. MARTIN'S STREET.** Being Chronicles of the Burney Family. By Constance Hill, Author of "Jane Austen, Her Home, and Her Friends," "Juniper Hall," etc. With numerous Illustrations by Ellen G. Hill, and reproductions of Contemporary Portraits, etc. Demy 8vo. 21s. net.

**STORY OF THE PRINCESS DES URSINS IN** SPAIN (Camarera-Mayor). By Constance Hill. With 12 Illustrations and a Photogravure Frontispiece. New Edition. Crown 8vo. 5s. net.

**MARIA EDGEWORTH AND HER CIRCLE** IN THE DAYS OF BONAPARTE AND BOURBON. By Constance Hill. Author of "Jane Austen : Her Homes and Her Friends," "Juniper Hall," "The House in St Martin's Street," etc. With numerous Illustrations by Ellen G. Hill and Reproductions of Contemporary Portraits, etc. Demy 8vo. (9 × 5½ inches). 21s. net.

**CESAR FRANCK :** A Study. Translated from the French of Vincent d'Indy, with an Introduction by Rosa Newmarch. Demy 8vo. (9 × 5¾ inches.) 7s. 6d. net.

**MEN AND LETTERS.** By Herbert Paul, M.P. Fourth Edition. Crown 8vo. 5s. net.

**ROBERT BROWNING :** Essays and Thoughts. By J. T. Nettleship. With Portrait. Crown 8vo. 5s. 6d. net. (Third Edition).

## NEW LETTERS OF THOMAS CARLYLE.

Edited and Annotated by ALEXANDAR CARLYLE, with Notes and an Introduction and numerous Illustrations. In Two Volumes. Demy 8vo. (9 × 5¾ inches.) 25s. net.

*Pall Mall Gazette.*—"To the portrait of the man, Thomas, these letters do really add value ; we can learn to respect and to like him more for the genuine goodness of his personality.

*Literary World.*—"It is then Carlyle, the nobly filial son, we see in these letters ; Carlyle, the generous and affectionate brother, the loyal and warm-hearted friend, . . . and above all, Carlyle as a tender and faithful lover of his wife."

*Daily Telegraph.*—"The letters are characteristic enough of the Carlyle we know : very picturesque and entertaining, full of extravagant emphasis, written, as a rule, at fever heat, eloquently rabid and emotional."

## NEW LETTERS AND MEMORIALS OF JANE

WELSH CARLYLE. A Collection of hitherto Unpublished Letters. Annotated by THOMAS CARLYLE, and Edited by ALEXANDER CARLYLE, with an Introduction by SIR JAMES CRICHTON BROWNE, M.D., LL.D., F.R.S., numerous Illustrations drawn in Lithography by T. R. WAY, and Photogravure Portraits from hitherto unreproduced Originals. In Two Vols. Demy 8vo. (9 × 5¾ inches.) 25s. net.

*Westminister Gazette.*—" Few letters in the language have in such perfection the qualities which good letters should possess. Frank, gay, brilliant, indiscreet, immensely clever, whimsical, and audacious, they reveal a character which, with whatever alloy of human infirmity, must endear itself to any reader of understanding."

*World.*—" Throws a deal of new light on the domestic relations of the Sage of Chelsea They also contain the full text of Mrs. Carlyle's fascinating journal, and her own 'humorous and quaintly candid' narrative of her first love-affair."

## THE LOVE LETTERS OF THOMAS CAR-

LYLE AND JANE WELSH. Edited by ALEXANDER CARLYLE, Nephew of THOMAS CARLYLE, editor of " New Letters and Memorials of Jane Welsh Carlyle," " New Letters of Thomas Carlyle," etc. With 2 Portraits in colour and numerous other Illustrations. Demy 8vo (9 × 5¾ inches). 2 vols. 25s. net.

## CARLYLE'S FIRST LOVE. Margaret Gordon—

Lady Bannerman. An account of her Life, Ancestry and Homes ; her Family and Friends. By R. C. ARCHIBALD. With 20 Portraits and Illustrations, including a Frontispiece in Colour. Demy 8vo (9 × 5¾ inches). 10s. 6d. net.

## EMILE ZOLA : NOVELIST AND REFORMER. An

Account of his Life, Work, and Influence. By E. A. VIZETELLY. With numerous Illustrations, Portraits, etc. Demy 8vo. 21s. net.

**MEMOIRS OF THE MARTYR KING :** being a detailed record of the last two years of the Reign of His Most Sacred Majesty King Charles the First, 1646-1648-9. Compiled by ALAN FEA. With upwards of 100 Photogravure Portraits and other Illustrations, including relics. Royal 4to. £5 5s. od. net.

**MEMOIRS OF A VANISHED GENERATION** 1811-1855. Edited by MRS. WARRENNE BLAKE. With numerous Illustrations. Demy 8vo. (9 x 5¾ inches.) 16s. net.

**THE KING'S GENERAL IN THE WEST,** being the Life of Sir Richard Granville, Baronet (1600-1659). By ROGER GRANVILLE, M.A., Sub-Dean of Exeter Cathedral. With Illustrations. Demy 8vo. (9 x 5¾ inches.) 10s. 6d. net.

**THE LIFE AND LETTERS OF ROBERT** STEPHEN HAWKER, sometime Vicar of Morwenstow in Cornwall. By C. E. BYLES. With numerous Illustrations by J. LEY PETHYBRIDGE and others. Demy 8vo. (9 × 5¾ inches.) 7s. 6d. net.

**THE LIFE OF WILLIAM BLAKE.** By ALEXANDER GILCHRIST, Edited with an Introduction by W. GRAHAM ROBERTSON. Numerous Reproductions from Blake's most characteristic and remarkable designs. Demy 8vo. (9 × 5¾ inches.) 10s. 6d. net. New Edition.

**GEORGE MEREDITH :** Some Characteristics. By RICHARD LE GALLIENNE. With a Bibliography (much enlarged) by JOHN LANE. Portrait, etc. Crown 8vo. 5s. net. Fifth Edition. Revised.

**A QUEEN OF INDISCRETIONS.** The Tragedy of Caroline of Brunswick, Queen of England. From the Italian of G. P. CLERICI. Translated by FREDERIC CHAPMAN. With numerous Illustrations reproduced from contemporary Portraits and Prints. Demy 8vo. (9 × 5¾ inches.) 21s. net.

**LETTERS AND JOURNALS OF SAMUEL** GRIDLEY HOWE. Edited by his Daughter LAURA E. RICHARDS. With Notes and a Preface by F. B. SANBORN, an Introduction by Mrs. JOHN LANE, and a Portrait. Demy 8vo (9 × 5¾ inches). 16s. net.

GRIEG AND HIS MUSIC. By H. T. FINCK,
Author of " Wagner and his Works," etc.   With Illustrations.
Demy 8vo.   (9 × 5¾ inches.)   7s. 6d. net.

EDWARD A. MACDOWELL : a Biography.   By
LAWRENCE GILMAN, Author of " Phases of Modern Music,"
" Strauss' 'Salome,'"  " The Music of To-morrow and Other
Studies,"  " Edward Macdowell," etc.   Profusely illustrated.
Crown 8vo.   5s. net.

THE LIFE OF ST. MARY MAGDALEN.
Translated from the Italian of an unknown Fourteenth-Century
Writer by VALENTINA HAWTREY.   With an Introductory Note by
VERNON LEE, and 14 Full-page Reproductions from the Old Masters.
Crown 8vo.   5s. net.

WILLIAM  MAKEPEACE  THACKERAY.  A
Biography by LEWIS MELVILLE.   With 2 Photogravures and
numerous other Illustrations.   Demy 8vo (9 × 5¾ inches).
25s. net.

A LATER PEPYS.  The Correspondence of Sir
William Weller Pepys, Bart., Master in Chancery, 1758-1825,
with Mrs. Chapone, Mrs. Hartley, Mrs. Montague, Hannah More,
William Franks, Sir James Macdonald, Major Rennell, Sir
Nathaniel Wraxall, and others.   Edited, with an Introduction and
Notes, by ALICE C. C. GAUSSEN.   With numerous Illustrations.
Demy 8vo.   (9 × 5¾ inches.)   In Two Volumes.   32s. net.

ROBERT LOUIS STEVENSON, AN ELEGY ;
AND  OTHER  POEMS,  MAINLY  PERSONAL.   By
RICHARD LE GALLIENNE.   Crown 8vo.   4s. 6d. net.

RUDYARD KIPLING : a Criticism,  By RICHARD
LE GALLIENNE.   With a Bibliography by JOHN LANE.   Crown
8vo.   3s. 6d. net.

THE LIFE OF W. J. FOX, Public Teacher and
Social Reformer, 1786-1864.   By the late RICHARD GARNETT,
C.B., LL.D., concluded by EDWARD GARNETT.   Demy 8vo.
(9 × 5¾ inches).   16s. net.

JOHN LANE, THE BODLEY HEAD, VIGO STREET, LONDON, W.

Lightning Source UK Ltd.
Milton Keynes UK
UKHW022307080223
416651UK00001B/306